# Machines & Motion

## Teacher Supplement

**1:1**

# Answers
## IN GENESIS™

**GOD'S
DESIGN®**

**4th Edition**
Debbie & Richard Lawrence

*God's Design® for Physical World*
*Machines & Motion Teacher Supplement*

Printed January 2016

Fourth edition. Copyright © 2008, 2016 by Debbie & Richard Lawrence

ISBN: 978-1-62691-464-3

Published by Answers in Genesis, 2800 Bullittsburg Church Rd., Petersburg KY 41080

Book designer: Diane King
Editors: Gary Vaterlaus

The publisher and authors have made every reasonable effort to ensure that the activities recommended in this book are safe when performed as instructed but assume no responsibility for any damage caused or sustained while conducting the experiments and activities. It is the parents', guardians', and/or teachers' responsibility to supervise all recommended activities.

Printed in China.

AnswersInGenesis.org  •  GodsDesign.com

# Welcome to GOD'S DESIGN®

## PHYSICAL WORLD

*God's Design for the Physical World* is a series that has been designed for use in teaching physical science to elementary and middle school students. It is divided into three books: *Heat and Energy*, *Machines and Motion*, and *Inventions and Technology*. Each book has 35 lessons including a final project that ties all of the lessons together.

In addition to the lessons, special features in each book include biographical information on interesting people as well as fun facts to make the subject more fun.

Although this is a complete curriculum, the information included here is just a beginning, so please feel free to add to each lesson as you see fit. A resource guide is included in the appendices to help you find additional information and resources. A list of supplies needed is included at the beginning of each lesson, while a master list of all supplies needed for the entire series can be found in the appendices.

Answer keys for all review questions, worksheets, quizzes, and the final exam are included here. Reproducible student worksheets and tests may be found in the digital download that comes with the purchase of the curriculum. You may download these files from GodsDesign.com/PhysicalWorld.

If you prefer the files on a CD-ROM, you can order that from Answers in Genesis at an additional cost by calling 800-778-3390.

If you wish to get through all three books of the *Physical World* series in one year, you should plan on covering approximately three lessons per week. The time required for each lesson varies depending on how much additional information you want to include, but you can plan on about 45 minutes per lesson.

If you wish to cover the material in more depth, you may add additional information and take a longer period of time to cover all the material or you could choose to do only one or two of the books in the series as a unit study.

## Why Teach Physical Science?

Maybe you hate science or you just hate teaching it. Maybe you love science but don't quite know how to teach it to your children. Maybe science just doesn't seem as important as some of those other subjects you need to teach. Maybe you need a little motivation. If any of these descriptions fits you, then please consider the following.

It is not uncommon to question the need to teach your kids hands-on science in elementary school. We could argue that the knowledge gained in science will be needed later in life in order for your children to be more productive and well-rounded adults. We could argue that teaching your children science also teaches them logical and inductive thinking and reasoning skills, which are tools they will need to be more successful. We could argue that science is a necessity in this technological world in which we live. While all of these arguments are true, not one of them is the real reason that we should teach our children science. The most important reason to teach science in elementary school is to give your children an understanding that God is our Creator, and the Bible can be trusted. Teaching science from a creation perspective is one of the best ways to reinforce your children's faith in God and to help them counter the evolutionary propaganda they face every day.

God is the Master Creator of everything. His handiwork is all around us. Our Great Creator put in place all of the laws of physics, biology, and chemistry. These laws were put here for us to see His wisdom and power. In science, we see the hand of God at work more than in any other subject. Romans 1:20 says, "For since the creation of the world His invisible attributes are clearly seen, being understood by the things that are made, even His eternal power and Godhead, so that they [men] are without excuse." We need to help our children see God as Creator of the world around them so they will be able to recognize God and follow Him.

The study of physical science helps us to understand and appreciate the amazing way everything God created works together. The study of energy helps us understand that God set up the universe with enough energy to sustain life and that He created the sun to replenish the energy used up each day. The study of friction and movement helps us appreciate the laws of motion and helps us understand how simple machines can be used to do big things. And finally, studying inventions and technology will not only help us understand the technological world in which we live, but will help us realize that God created man to be creative just like Him.

It's fun to teach physics. It's interesting too. Energy and motion are all around us. We use technology and inventions every day. Finally, teaching physics is easy. You won't have to try to find strange materials for experiments or do dangerous things to learn about physics. Physics is as close as your child's toy box or the telephone—it's the rainbow in the sky and it's the light bulb in the lamp. So enjoy your study of the physical world.

# How Do I Teach Science?

In order to teach any subject you need to understand how people learn. People learn in different ways. Most people, and children in particular, have a dominant or preferred learning style in which they absorb and retain information more easily.

**If a student's dominant style is:**

| |
| --- |
| **Auditory**<br>He needs not only to hear the information but he needs to hear himself say it. This child needs oral presentation as well as oral drill and repetition. |
| **Visual**<br>She needs things she can see. This child responds well to flashcards, pictures, charts, models, etc. |
| **Kinesthetic**<br>He needs active participation. This child remembers best through games, hands-on activities, experiments, and field trips. |

Also, some people are more relational while others are more analytical. The relational student needs to know why this subject is important, and how it will affect him personally. The analytical student, however, wants just the facts.

If you are trying to teach more than one student, you will probably have to deal with more than one learning style. Therefore, you need to present your lessons in several different ways so that each student can grasp and retain the information.

## Grades 3–8

The first part of each lesson should be completed by all upper elementary and junior high students. This is the main part of the lesson containing a reading section, a hands-on activity that reinforces the ideas in the reading section (blue box), and a review section that provides review questions and application questions.

## Grades 6–8

In addition, for middle school/junior high age students, we provide a "Challenge" section that contains more challenging material as well as additional activities and projects for older students (green box).

We have included periodic biographies to help your students appreciate the great men and women who have gone before us in the field of science.

We suggest a threefold approach to each lesson:

## Introduce the topic

We give a brief description of the facts. Frequently you will want to add more information than the essentials given in this book. In addition to reading this section aloud (or having older children read it on their own), you may wish to do one or more of the following:

- Read a related book with your students.
- Write things down to help your visual learners.
- Give some history of the subject. We provide some historical sketches to help you, but you may want to add more.
- Ask questions to get your students thinking about the subject.

## Make observations and do experiments

- Hands-on projects are suggested for each lesson. This part of each lesson may require help from the teacher.
- Have your students perform the activity by themselves whenever possible.

## Review

- The "What did we learn?" section has review questions.
- The "Taking it further" section encourages students to
  - Draw conclusions
  - Make applications of what was learned
  - Add extended information to what was covered in the lesson
- The "FUN FACT" section adds fun or interesting information.

By teaching all three parts of the lesson, you will be presenting the material in a way that children with any learning style can both relate to and remember.

Also, this approach relates directly to the scientific method and will help your students think more scientifically. The *scientific method* is just a way to examine a subject logically and learn from it. Briefly, the steps of the scientific method are:

1. Learn about a topic.
2. Ask a question.
3. Make a hypothesis (a good guess).
4. Design an experiment to test your hypothesis.
5. Observe the experiment and collect data.
6. Draw conclusions. (Does the data support your hypothesis?)

Note: It's okay to have a "wrong hypothesis." That's how we learn. Be sure to help your students understand why they sometimes get a different result than expected.

Our lessons will help your students begin to approach problems in a logical, scientific way.

# How Do I Teach Creation vs. Evolution?

We are constantly bombarded by evolutionary ideas about the earth in books, movies, museums, and even commercials. These raise many questions: Do physical processes support evolutionary theories? Do physical laws support an old earth? Do changes in the magnetic field support an old earth? The Bible answers these questions, and this book accepts the historical accuracy of the Bible as written. We believe this is the only way we can teach our children to trust that everything God says is true.

There are five common views of the origins of life and the age of the earth:

| Historical biblical account | Progressive creation | Gap theory | Theistic evolution | Naturalistic evolution |
|---|---|---|---|---|
| Each day of creation in Genesis is a normal day of about 24 hours in length, in which God created everything that exists. The earth is only thousands of years old, as determined by the genealogies in the Bible. | The idea that God created various creatures to replace other creatures that died out over millions of years. Each of the days in Genesis represents a long period of time (day-age view) and the earth is billions of years old. | The idea that there was a long, long time between what happened in Genesis 1:1 and what happened in Genesis 1:2. During this time, the "fossil record" was supposed to have formed, and millions of years of earth history supposedly passed. | The idea that God used the process of evolution over millions of years (involving struggle and death) to bring about what we see today. | The view that there is no God and evolution of all life forms happened by purely naturalistic processes over billions of years. |

Any theory that tries to combine the evolutionary time frame with creation presupposes that death entered the world before Adam sinned, which contradicts what God has said in His Word. The view that the earth (and its "fossil record") is hundreds of millions of years old damages the gospel message. God's completed creation was "very good" at the end of the sixth day (Genesis 1:31). Death entered this perfect paradise *after* Adam disobeyed God's command. It was the punishment for Adam's sin (Genesis 2:16–17; 3:19; Romans 5:12–19). Thorns appeared when God cursed the ground because of Adam's sin (Genesis 3:18).

The first animal death occurred when God killed at least one animal, shedding its blood, to make clothes for Adam and Eve (Genesis 3:21). If the earth's "fossil record" (filled with death, disease, and thorns) formed over millions of years before Adam appeared (and before he sinned), then death no longer would be the penalty for sin. Death, the "last enemy" (1 Corinthians 15:26), diseases (such as cancer), and thorns would instead be part of the original creation that God labeled "very good." No, it is clear that the "fossil record" formed sometime *after* Adam sinned—not many millions of years before. Most fossils were formed as a result of the worldwide Genesis Flood.

When viewed from a biblical perspective, the scientific evidence clearly supports a recent creation by God, and not naturalistic evolution and millions of years. The volume of evidence supporting the biblical creation account is substantial and cannot be adequately covered in this book. If you would like more information on this topic, please see the resource guide in the appendices To help get you started, just a few examples of evidence supporting biblical creation are given below:

**The Truth**: Much of what scientists observe directly contradicts the ideas of evolution. Certain physical properties have been observed and tested to the point that they have been declared to be physical laws. The first law of thermodynamics states that matter and energy cannot be created or destroyed; they can only change form. There is no mechanism in nature for creating either energy or matter. Therefore, evolutionists cannot explain how all of the matter and energy in the universe came to be. This is a topic most evolutionists tend to ignore. The Bible tells us that God created it all and set it in motion.

The second law of thermodynamics states that all systems move toward a state of maximum entropy. This means that everything moves toward total disorganization and equilibrium. Heat moves from an area of higher temperature to an area of lower temperature, and organized systems become disorganized. For example, an organized system of cells that makes up a living creature quickly becomes disorganized when that creature dies. A house left to itself will eventually crumble into dust. Everything around us says that without intervention, chaos and disorganization result. Evolutionists, however, believe that by accident, simple molecules and simple organisms combined to form more complex molecules and organisms. This flies in the face of the second law of thermodynamics and everything that is observed to happen naturally. The changes required for the formation of the universe, the planet earth and life, all from disorder, run counter to the physical laws we see at work today. There is no known mechanism to harness the raw energy of the universe and generate the specified complexity we see all around us.[1]

A third physical property that contradicts evolution is the small amount of helium in the atmosphere. Helium is naturally generated by the radioactive decay of elements in the earth's crust. Because helium is so light, it quickly moves up through the rocks and into the atmosphere. Helium is entering the atmosphere at about 13 million atoms per square inch per second (67 grams/second). Some helium atoms are also escaping the atmosphere into space, but the amount of helium escaping into space is only about 1/40th the amount entering the atmosphere. So, the overall amount of helium in the atmosphere is continually increasing. If you assume that helium cannot enter the atmosphere any other way, which is a reasonable assumption, then the amount of helium in the atmosphere indicates that the earth could be no more than two million years old, which is much less than the billions of years needed for evolution. This is a maximum age—the actual age could be much less since this calculation assumes that the original atmosphere had no helium whatsoever. Also, helium could have been released at a much greater rate during the time after the Genesis Flood. Therefore, the amount of helium in the atmosphere indicates a much younger earth than evolutionists claim.[2]

[1] John D. Morris, *The Young Earth* (Colorado Springs: Creation Life Publishers, 1994), p. 43. See also www.answersingenesis.org/go/thermodynamics.

[2] Ibid., pp. 83–85.

**Evolutionary Myth:** Changes in the earth's magnetic field indicate an earth that is billions of years old.

**The Truth:** Most scientists agree on some fundamental facts concerning the earth's magnetic field. The earth is a giant electromagnet. The earth is surrounded by a magnetic field that is believed to be generated by current flowing through the interior of the earth. And there is evidence that the magnetic field of the earth has reversed several times. Also, nearly everyone agrees that the magnetic field is decreasing. The disagreement between evolutionists and creationists concerns how long it takes for the earth's magnetic field to change and what caused or causes the changes. Evolutionists believe that the magnetic field slowly decreases over time, reverses, and then slowly increases again. There are some serious problems with this idea. First, when the magnetic field is very low the earth would have no protection from very harmful radiation from the sun. This would be detrimental to life on earth. Second, at the current rate of decay, the magnetic field of the earth would lose half its energy about every 1,460 years. If the rate of decay is constant, the magnetic field would have been so strong only 20,000 years ago that it would have caused massive heating in the earth's crust and would have killed all life on earth. This supports the idea of an earth that is only about 6,000 years old, as taught in the Bible.

Creationists believe that the magnetic field reversals happened very quickly, and that the decay rate is fairly constant. One study of a lava flow indicated that reversals occurred in only 15 days. Thus, the reversals likely happened as a result of the Genesis Flood when the tectonic plates were moving and the earth's crust was in upheaval.[3]

[3] Ibid., pp. 74–83.

Despite the claims of many scientists, if you examine the evidence objectively, it is obvious that evolution and millions of years have not been proven. You can be confident that if you teach that what the Bible says is true, you won't go wrong. Instill in your student a confidence in the truth of the Bible in all areas. If scientific thought seems to contradict the Bible, realize that scientists often make mistakes, but God does not lie. At one time scientists believed that the earth was the center of the universe, that living things could spring from non-living things, and that bloodletting was good for the body. All of these were believed to be scientific facts but have since been disproved, but the Word of God remains true. If we use modern "science" to interpret the Bible, what will happen to our faith in God's Word when scientists change their theories yet again?

# Integrating the Seven C's

The Seven C's is a framework in which all of history, and the future to come, can be placed. As we go through our daily routines we may not understand how the details of life connect with the truth that we find in the Bible. This is also the case for students. When discussing the importance of the Bible you may find yourself telling students that the Bible is relevant in everyday activities. But how do we help the younger generation see that? The Seven C's are intended to help.

The Seven C's can be used to develop a biblical worldview in students, young or old. Much more than entertaining stories and religious teachings, the Bible has real connections to our everyday life. It may be hard, at first, to see how many connections there are, but with practice, the daily relevance of God's Word will come alive. Let's look at the Seven C's of History and how each can be connected to what the students are learning.

## Creation

God perfectly created the heavens, the earth, and all that is in them in six normal-length days around 6,000 years ago.

This teaching is foundational to a biblical worldview and can be put into the context of any subject. In science, the amazing design that we see in nature—whether in the veins of a leaf or the complexity of your hand—is all the handiwork of God. Virtually all of the lessons in *God's Design for Science* can be related to God's creation of the heavens and earth.

Other contexts include:

*Natural laws*—any discussion of a law of nature naturally leads to God's creative power.

*DNA and information*—the information in every living thing was created by God's supreme intelligence.

*Mathematics*—the laws of mathematics reflect the order of the Creator.

*Biological diversity*—the distinct kinds of animals that we see were created during the Creation Week, not as products of evolution.

*Art*—the creativity of man is demonstrated through various art forms.

*History*—all time scales can be compared to the biblical time scale extending back about 6,000 years.

*Ecology*—God has called mankind to act as stewards over His creation.

## Corruption

After God completed His perfect creation, Adam disobeyed God by eating the forbidden fruit. As a result, sin and death entered the world, and the world has been in decay since that time. This point is evident throughout the world that we live in. The struggle for survival in animals, the death of loved ones, and the violence all around us are all examples of the corrupting influence of sin.

Other contexts include:

*Genetics*—the mutations that lead to diseases, cancer, and variation within populations are the result of corruption.

*Biological relationships*—predators and parasites result from corruption.

*History*—wars and struggles between mankind, exemplified in the account of Cain and Abel, are a result of sin.

## Catastrophe

God was grieved by the wickedness of mankind and judged this wickedness with a global Flood. The Flood covered the entire surface of the earth and killed all air-breathing creatures that were not aboard the Ark. The eight people and the animals aboard the Ark replenished the earth after God delivered them from the catastrophe.

The catastrophe described in the Bible would naturally leave behind much evidence. The studies of geology and of the biological diversity of animals on the planet are two of the most obvious applications of this event. Much of scientific understanding is based on how a scientist views the events of the Genesis Flood.

Other contexts include:

*Biological diversity*—all of the birds, mammals, and other air-breathing animals have populated the earth from the original kinds which left the Ark.

*Geology*—the layers of sedimentary rock seen in road-cuts, canyons, and other geologic features are testaments to the global Flood.

*Geography*—features like mountains, valleys, and plains were formed as the floodwaters receded.

*Physics*—rainbows are a perennial sign of God's faithfulness and His pledge to never flood the entire earth again.

*Fossils*—Most fossils are a result of the Flood rapidly burying plants and animals.

*Plate tectonics*—the rapid movement of the earth's plates likely accompanied the Flood.

*Global warming/Ice Age*—both of these items are likely a result of the activity of the Flood. The warming we are experiencing today has been present since the peak of the Ice Age (with variations over time).

## Confusion

God commanded Noah and his descendants to spread across the earth. The refusal to obey this command and the building of the tower at Babel caused God to judge this sin. The common language of the people was confused and they spread across the globe as groups with a common language. All people are truly of "one blood" as descendants of Noah and, originally, Adam.

The confusion of the languages led people to scatter across the globe. As people settled in new areas, the traits they carried with them became concentrated in those populations. Traits like dark skin were beneficial in the tropics while other traits benefited populations in northern climates, and distinct people groups, not races, developed.

Other contexts include:

*Genetics*—the study of human DNA has shown that there is little difference in the genetic makeup of the so-called "races."

*Languages*—there are about seventy language groups from which all modern languages have developed.

*Archaeology*—the presence of common building structures, like pyramids, around the world confirms the biblical account.

*Literature*—recorded and oral records tell of similar events relating to the Flood and the dispersion at Babel.

## Christ

God did not leave mankind without a way to be redeemed from its sinful state. The Law was given to Moses to show how far away man is from God's standard of perfection. Rather than the sacrifices, which only covered sins, people needed a Savior to take away their sin. This was accomplished when Jesus Christ came to earth to live a perfect life and, by that obedience, was able to be the sacrifice to satisfy God's wrath for all who believe.

The deity of Christ and the amazing plan that was set forth before the foundation of the earth is the core of Christian doctrine. The earthly life of Jesus was the fulfillment of many prophecies and confirms the truthfulness of the Bible. His miracles and presence in human form demonstrate that God is both intimately concerned with His creation and able to control it in an absolute way.

Other contexts include:

*Psychology*—popular secular psychology teaches of the inherent goodness of man, but Christ has lived the only perfect life. Mankind needs a Savior to redeem it from its unrighteousness.

*Biology*—Christ's virgin birth demonstrates God's sovereignty over nature.

*Physics*—turning the water into wine and the feeding of the five thousand demonstrate Christ's deity and His sovereignty over nature.

*History*—time is marked (in the western world) based on the birth of Christ despite current efforts to change the meaning.

*Art*—much art is based on the life of Christ and many of the masters are known for these depictions, whether on canvas or in music.

## Cross

Because God is perfectly just and holy, He must punish sin. The sinless life of Jesus Christ was offered as a substitutionary sacrifice for all of those who will repent and put their faith in the Savior. After His death on the Cross, He defeated death by rising on the third day and is now seated at the right hand of God.

The events surrounding the Crucificion and Ressurection have a most significant place in the life of Christians.

Though there is no way to scientifically prove the Ressurection, there is likewise no way to prove the stories of evolutionary history. These are matters of faith founded in the truth of God's Word and His character. The eyewitness testimony of over 500 people and the written Word of God provide the basis for our belief.

Other contexts include:

*Biology*—the biological details of the Crucifixion can be studied alongside the anatomy of the human body.

*History*—the use of Crucifixion as a method of punishment was short-lived in historical terms and not known at the time it was prophesied.

*Art*—the Crucifixion and Resurrection have inspired many wonderful works of art.

## Consummation

God, in His great mercy, has promised that He will restore the earth to its original state—a world without death, suffering, war, and disease. The corruption introduced by Adam's sin will be removed. Those who have repented and put their trust in the completed work of Christ on the Cross will experience life in this new heaven and earth. We will be able to enjoy and worship God forever in a perfect place.

This future event is a little more difficult to connect with academic subjects. However, the hope of a life in God's presence and in the absence of sin can be inserted in discussions of human conflict, disease, suffering, and sin in general.

Other contexts include:

*History*—in discussions of war or human conflict the coming age offers hope.

*Biology*—the violent struggle for life seen in the predator-prey relationships will no longer taint the earth.

*Medicine*—while we struggle to find cures for diseases and alleviate the suffering of those enduring the effects of the Curse, we ultimately place our hope in the healing that will come in the eternal state.

The preceding examples are given to provide ideas for integrating the Seven C's of History into a broad range of curriculum activities. We would recommend that you give your students, and yourself, a better understanding of the Seven C's framework by using AiG's *Answers for Kids* curriculum. The first seven lessons of this curriculum cover the Seven C's and will establish a solid understanding of the true history, and future, of the universe. Full lesson plans, activities, and student resources are provided in the curriculum set.

We also offer bookmarks displaying the Seven C's and a wall chart. These can be used as visual cues for the students to help them recall the information and integrate new learning into its proper place in a biblical worldview.

Even if you use other curricula, you can still incorporate the Seven C's teaching into those. Using this approach will help students make firm connections between biblical events and every aspect of the world around them, and they will begin to develop a truly biblical worldview and not just add pieces of the Bible to what they learn in "the real world."

# Unit 1
# Mechanical Forces

# 1 Introduction to Mechanical Energy

Let's get moving

## Supply list

Tennis ball      String

Tennis racquet or baseball bat
Copy of "Types of Motion" worksheet

## Types of Motion worksheet

| Activity | Observed motion | Forces affecting movement of ball |
|---|---|---|
| 1. Roll a tennis ball along the ground. | **Straight line** | **Forward motion from hand, then slowed down by contact with the surface** |
| 2. Hold a tennis ball as high as you can and then drop it. | **Straight down** | **Gravity** |
| 3. Hit a tennis ball with a tennis racquet or baseball bat into an open area. | **Arc** | **Forward motion from racquet, gravity** |
| 4. Hit the tennis ball against a wall (with no windows). | **Arc with a reflection of movement from wall** | **Forward motion from racquet, gravity, push from wall** |
| 5. Tie a string around the ball and swing it around your head. Be sure that no one is standing near you. After a few rotations, release the string. | **Circular, then an arc in a straight line** | **Pull from your arm, gravity** |

- Did the ball move faster when you rolled it or when you hit it with a racquet or bat? **The ball will move faster when hit by the racquet.**
- What happened to the ball on a string when you let go of it? **The ball on a string went flying in a straight line, but fell in an arc.**
- Why didn't it keep spinning? **It no longer had a force pulling it toward the center.**

## What did we learn?

- What is mechanics? **The study of motion or moving objects.**

- What is energy? **The ability to perform work.**
- What are some ways that objects move? **In straight lines, in arcs, in circles, etc.**

## Taking it further

- What force greatly affects motion on earth? **Gravity.**
- List three or more ways that mechanical advantage is being used around you. **Door hinges, wheels, engines, nut crackers, scissors, automobiles, etc.**

# 2 Potential & Kinetic Energy

## Ready to move

## Supply list

Rubber bands          Paper

Book                  Drawing compass

## Supplies for Challenge

Ruler or yardstick

Copy of "Calculating Energy" worksheet

## Conversion of Energy

- Hold a book a few inches above the table and drop it. Describe the conversion of energy that just occurred. **Your kinetic energy was converted into potential energy as you lifted the book. That potential energy was converted into kinetic energy as the book fell to the table. Finally, some of the mechanical energy was converted into sound energy as the book hit the table.**

- Describe the conversion of energy that is occurring as you shoot a rubber band. **You are using kinetic energy to stretch the rubber band. This kinetic energy is converted to potential energy in the stretched rubber band. The potential energy is then converted back into kinetic energy as the rubber band returns to its normal size and flies through the air.**

## What did we learn?

- What is potential energy? **Energy that is stored and ready to be used.**

- What is kinetic energy? **Energy that is being used.**

- Give several examples of objects with potential energy. **Anything that is above ground level, including a skier at the top of a hill, a bird on a roof, a wound spring, a stretched cord, etc.**

- Give several examples of objects with kinetic energy. **Anything that is moving, including a dog running, a car driving down the street, a ball sailing through the air, etc.**

## Taking it further

- Describe the transfer of energy between kinetic and potential energy that occurs during a roller coaster ride. **Kinetic energy is used to move the car to the top of a hill where it now has maximum potential energy. As the car moves down the hill this potential energy is converted into kinetic energy. At the bottom of the hill all of the potential energy has been changed and the car has** maximum kinetic energy. As the car moves up the next hill, the kinetic energy is again converted into potential energy.

- Explain how a wind-up clock uses potential and mechanical energy. **Kinetic energy from your hand is used to wind up or coil a spring inside the clock, thus giving it potential energy. The spring slowly unwinds, converting the potential energy into mechanical energy as the gears inside the clock move the hands of the clock.**

## Challenge: Calculating Energy

- If you hold the student manual 0.5 meters above the table: **P.E. = 0.4 kg x 9.8 m/s² x 0.5 m = 1.96 J.**

- If you hold the student manual 1 meter above the floor: **P.E. = 0.4 kg x 9.8 m/s² x 1 m = 3.92 J.**

  **(Your answers may differ depending on the height of the book.)**

- Kinetic energy of the softball: **Kinetic energy of the softgball—K.E. = 0.5 x 2 kg x (5 m/s)² = 25 J; K.E. = 0.5 x 2 kg x (10 m/sec)² = 100 J.**

- **The stopping distance of the car is four times greater at 80 kph than at 40 kph because the kinetic energy is four times greater.**

## Challenge: Calculating Energy worksheet

1. A 3 kg rock is perched on an outcropping 20 meters above the ground. How much potential energy does it have? **U = mgh = 3 kg x 9.8 m/s² x 20 m = 588 J.**

2. If you lift a 16 kg child from the floor to her bed, which is 1 meter high, how much have you increased her potential energy? **U=mgh = 16 kg x 9.8 m/s² x 1 m = 156.8 J.**

3. How does the potential energy of an airplane change as it takes off and flies? **As the airplane leaves the ground the potential energy increases as the altitude increases.**

4. How does the potential energy of the same airplane change as it lands? **As the altitude decreases, the potential energy decreases.**

5. What is the kinetic energy of a 0.2 kg softball thrown at 5 meters/second? **K = ½mv² = 0.5 x 0.2 kg x 25 m²/s² = 2.5 J.**

6.  What is the kinetic energy of the same softball thrown at 10 meters/second? **K = ½mv² = 0.5 x 0.2 kg x 100 m²/s² = 10J.**

7.  A car is traveling at 24 meters/second. If it has a mass of 900 kg, what is its kinetic energy? **K = ½mv² = 0.5 x 900 kg x 576 m²/s² = 259,200 J.**

8.  If the same car is traveling at 12 meters/second what is its kinetic energy? **K = ½mv² = 0.5 x 900 kg x 144 m²/s² = 64,800 J.**

9.  How does the kinetic energy of an airplane change as it takes off? **As the plane's speed increases (as it accelerates) the kinietic energy increases, but it increases rapidly since the velocity is squared in the calculation. If the speed doubles, the kinetic energy goes up by a factor of 4.**

10. How does the kinetic energy of an airplane change as it lands? **As the plane's speed decreases (as it adecelerates) the kinietic energy decreases, but it decreases rapidly since the velocity is squared in the calculation. If the speed is cut in half, the kinetic energy decreases by a factor of 4.**

# 3  Conservation of Energy

## Can it be used up?

## Supply list

Copy of "Energy Conservation" worksheet

Toy car                    Books

Piece of wood or cardboard

## Energy Conservation worksheet

*   Activity 1: **The car moves until all of the usable energy is lost. Your push is mechanical energy that is transferred to the car. The mechanical kinetic energy of the car is transformed into heat and sound from the friction between the wheels and the floor, the wheels and the axles, and between the car and the air molecules.**

*   Activity 2: **When you lifted the car to the top of the ramp, your mechanical kinetic energy was converted into potential energy from gravity. That potential energy was converted into kinetic energy as the car rolled down the ramp and across the floor. The car's mechanical energy was again converted into heat and sound energy due to friction.**

*   Activity 3: **Mechanical energy of pushing air across your vocal cords is converted into sound energy. The sound energy is eventually lost due to friction with air molecules. If you want to take the energy conversions back even further, the mechanical energy in your throat came from the chemical energy in your food and the chemical energy in your food came from the light energy from the sun that was converted into chemical energy by plants.**

## What did we learn?

*   What is the law of conservation of energy? **Energy cannot be created or destroyed, it can only change forms.**

*   What is the first law of thermodynamics? **In a closed system, energy can neither be created nor destroyed, only transformed or transferred; energy is conserved.**

*   What is the law of conservation of mass? **Matter cannot be created or destroyed in physical and chemical reactions, but only changes form.**

*   What happens to mechanical energy that causes a moving object to slow down and eventually stop? **The mechanical energy is converted into heat energy through friction as well as sound.**

## Taking it further

*   If we lived in a world with no friction, what would happen to a toy car when you pushed it across the floor? **It would slide until it collided with something else, then it would bounce back toward you. The wheels would probably not turn because they would not have friction to grip the floor and turn.**

*   What famous equation did Einstein publish that explains how mass and energy are related? **E = mc², which shows that mass can be converted into energy.**

*   Based on your observations, what is the most likely final form of energy? **Heat is the end product of most activities.**

## Challenge: Joule's Experiment

*   **The movement of the paddle increases the movement of the water molecules. The kinetic energy of the paddle is transferred to the water molecules. Temperature is a measure of the average kinetic energy of the molecules.**

# 4 Conservation of Momentum

## Moving masses

## Supply list

6 Marbles

Golf ball

Ping-pong ball

Dominoes

Hardback book

## Supplies for Challenge

2 long wooden pencils

Thread

Pen knife

5 small and 5 large glass beads

Ruler

Calculator

4 cans

## Observing Momentum

- What happened when the moving marble collided with the still marbles? **The moving marble stopped moving and the last marble in the row began moving.**

- Why did this happen? **The momentum from the first marble was transferred to the second marble and then to the third and so on until the last marble began to move away.**

- What would you expect to see happen if you rolled two marbles together toward the stationary marbles? Try this and see what happens. **You should observe the last two marbles begin to move away as the momentum from the first moving marble transfers to the last marble in the row, and the momentum from the second moving marble transfers to the second to last marble in the row.**

- Set up a row of dominoes in a way that if the first one falls, they will all fall in turn. Predict what will happen if you roll a ping pong ball toward the first domino. Gently roll the ball toward the dominoes. What did you observe? **If the dominoes are heavy, it is likely that the ping pong ball just bounced off.**

- What do you think will happen if you roll a golf ball toward the dominoes instead? Try it and see. **The golf ball should knock over the first domino, which in turn knocks over the other dominoes.**

- Why was the ping pong ball unable to knock over the dominoes? **It did not have enough mass, and therefore did not have enough momentum to knock over the first domino.**

- Why was the golf ball able to knock over the dominoes? **It had more mass and therefore more momentum.**

## What did we learn?

- What is momentum? **The movement of a mass in a particular direction.**

- What two quantities affect an object's momentum? **Its mass and velocity.**

- What is the law of conservation of momentum? **The momentum of a system after a collision must be the same as the momentum before the collision.**

## Taking it further

- If a large football player and a small soccer player are running toward each other, what is likely to happen to the speed and direction of each player when they collide? **The larger player will be slowed down slightly, while the smaller player will be stopped completely and will be moved in the opposite direction.**

- What will happen if you shoot a penny across a smooth table into a stationary penny? **The first penny will stop and the second penny will accelerate as the momentum of the first penny is transferred to the second penny— try it.**

- How might a ping pong ball be made to knock over a heavy domino? **If it has more velocity, it will have more momentum, so if you could shoot it at a high enough velocity, it will have enough momentum to overcome the domino's inertia.**

- If a golf ball is rolled very slowly, will it still knock over the dominoes? **No, if it rolls slowly enough it will not have enough momentum to overcome the domino's inertia.**

## Challenge: Calculating Momentum

- $p_1 = 50$ kg x 4 m/s = 200 kg-m/s; $p_2 = 45$kg x 4 m/s = 180 kg-m/s; **The boy has more momentum because he has more mass.**

- $p_3 = 5$ kg x 8 m/s = 40 kg-m/s; $p_4 = 0.05$ kg x1000 m/s = 50 kg-m/s; **The bullet has more momentum than the bowling ball because of its greater velocity.**

# 5 Force

## Tug of war

## Supply list

Sewing thread      2 pencils

Modeling clay      Rope

Kite string

## Supplies for Challenge

Bathroom scale

Copy of "Sum of Forces" worksheet

## Testing Forces

- Testing Tensile Strength: How difficult was this to do? **It should not be too difficult with most sewing thread.**

- Were you able to break the string? **Depending on the string, you may or may not have been able to break the string.**

- If you and your partner pull as hard as you can, do you break the piece of rope? **Probably not.**

- Testing Buoyancy: You can test buoyancy by shaping modeling clay into various shapes. Which shapes will float? Which shapes will sink? Why do some shapes sink and others float? **Different shapes push different amounts of water away. If the weight of water displaced is equal to the weight of the clay, the clay will float. If it is less than the weight of the clay, the clay will sink. Spreading out the clay so that it has a greater surface area spreads out the weight and allows it to displace enough water for it to float.**

## What did we learn?

- What is mechanical force? **A push or a pull on an object.**

- What is tension? **A continuous pull on an object.**

- What is tensile strength? **The amount of tension that an object can withstand.**

- What is buoyancy? **The force exerted by a gas or a liquid that is displaced.**

## Taking it further

- What are some of the forces that are being exerted during a basketball game? **The players are pushing on the ball; they are pushing on the floor with their feet; sometimes they pull down on the hoop and sometimes they push or pull each other. The floor is pushing back on the players and the ball when it bounces.**

- Why can you float more easily in the ocean than you can in a fresh water swimming pool? **The salt in the ocean makes it denser and thus heavier. Therefore, you displace a greater weight in salt water than in fresh water so you are more buoyant.**

- What would happen to a boat that was moving upstream at the same speed as the current was moving downstream? **The boat would remain in one place.**

- What are the forces exerted on and by a skier moving downhill? **The skier exerts some downward and backward force on his/her skis and poles; this pushes the skier forward. Then, gravity pulls down on the skier, causing him/her to accelerate downhill. The skis push down on the snow and the snow pushes up on the skis.**

## Challenge: Sum of Forces worksheet

- Boat 1: **Upstream at 5 km/hr.**

- Boat 2: **Downstream at 13 km/hr.**

- Boat 3: **Diagonally across and downstream at 5 km/hr.**

- **If your child knows about the Pythagorean theorem, the direction of the boat is the hypotenuse of a triangle with sides representing the direction of the boat and the direction of the current.**

# 6 Friction

## Opposing movement

## Supply list

Copy of "Friction" worksheet

Block of wood      Rubber band

Cup hook      Sandpaper

Ruler      Spring scale (optional)

## Friction worksheet

- Which surface allowed the block to move the easiest? **The block should move easiest over the smooth surface.**
- Which surface most resisted the movement of the block? **The sandpaper most likely gave the most resistance.**
- Was it easier to keep the block moving once it was started than to get it started to begin with? In other words, was the rubber band stretched further to get it moving initially than it was to keep it moving? **It is easier to keep a block moving than to get it started.**
- Why did it take more effort to get the block of wood started on the sandpaper than it did on the smooth surface? **The sandpaper has more friction.**

## What did we learn?

- What is friction? **A force that resists movement.**
- What is the cause of friction? **The rubbing of two surfaces.**
- How can friction be useful? **It is necessary for walking, driving a car, and holding onto objects. It stops your ball from rolling away forever, etc.**

- How can friction be damaging? **Usually it is damaging because friction produces heat and too much heat can melt objects.**

## Taking it further

- When would street maintenance people try to increase friction on the streets? **When the streets are covered with ice and snow.**
- How do they try to increase the friction? **Either by melting the ice and snow with salt or other chemicals, or they increase friction by adding sand or gravel to the top of the ice and snow. They also remove as much of the ice and snow as they can with snowplows.**
- Why do drag racers use very wide treadless tires in a race? **This increases the amount of rubber in contact with the road, thus increasing the friction and giving the driver greater control at high speeds.**

## Challenge: Reducing friction

Some possible ideas for reducing friction include spreading oil on the surface, covering the surface with a smoother substance such as aluminum foil, or covering the bottom of the block of wood with a smoother/slippery substance.

# 7 Work

## Everyone has to do it

## Supply list

3 identical boxes with different objects inside

## Supplies for Challenge

Scale (bathroom scale)     Meter stick
Copy of "Work Calculation" worksheet

## Performing Work

### Activity 1:

- Which box required the most force to lift? Return that box to the floor and lift the third box to waist level. Of the three boxes, which one required the most force to lift? **The heaviest box will require the most force to lift.**
- Which box required you to do the most work to lift it? **You performed the most work when you lifted the heaviest box because work is force times height. Since you lifted all three boxes the same height the greatest work is done with the greatest force.**

### Activity 2:

- Which action required you to do more work? **Lifting the box to a higher position required more work.**

### Activity 3:

- How much work are you doing to hold the box? **Once you have lifted the box, you are no longer performing work because you are not moving the box any distance.**

## What did we learn?

- What is the scientific definition of work? **Force times distance—the force needed to move an object a certain distance.**
- Force is directly related to what physical property? **The mass of the object.**

## Taking it further

- Does work always have to be done in a vertical direction? **No, work is done when an applied force causes an object to change position.**

- If one student pushes very hard on a wall and a second student picks up a pencil, which student is doing the most work? **The second student is the only one doing any work, because the wall does not move. Therefore, the first student does not accomplish any work.**
- Is there any work being done as you coast downhill on your bike? **Yes, the force of gravity is pulling you and your bike down the hill so work is being done even if you are not pedaling.**
- Is there any work being done as a space probe moves through space? **No, there is no force being applied to the space probe, so no work is being done even though the** probe is moving. This is an unusual case. On earth, movement generally does not continue without some kind of force continually being applied because air resistance is continually slowing objects down. In space, once an object is set in motion it continues in motion indefinitely.

## Challenge: Work Calculation worksheet

- **Answers will vary with the weight of the boxes and the heights lifted. Lifting the heaviest box over the greatest distance results in the most work done. When weight is not moved, no work is done.**

# 8   Power

## Getting the job done quickly

## Supply list

Copy of "Power Scavenger Hunt"

## Supplies for Challenge

Copy of "Calculating Power" worksheet

## Power Scavenger Hunt

- Power requirements will vary depending on your appliances.
- Types of work performed:

  Washing Machine – **Moving clothes through the water**

  Hair Dryer – **Heating and moving air molecules**

  Car engine – **Moving pistons up and down to move the wheels of the car**

  Electric stove – **Electrons moving through the heating elements cause them to heat up**

  Lawn mower – **Blades are made to move quickly to cut the grass**

  Vacuum cleaner – **Air moves and often a beater brush moves to cause dirt particles to move into the machine**

  Toaster – **Electrons moving through the heating coils causes them to heat up**

  Computer – **Electrons moving through the circuits causes them to perform mathematical functions and other computations**

- Microwave oven – **Electromagnetic waves cause water molecules to move back and forth, heating the food**

- Which item in your house requires the most power? **Although probably not in your house, your car uses the most power**
- Explain how these items help you or your family save time. **The power of the motors can often do the task faster than your body can. Also, many of these appliances can do the task automatically while you do something else. So even if it is not faster, you save time because all you have to do is start the machine.**

## What did we learn?

- What is the scientific definition of power? **Amount of work done in a given period of time.**
- How do machines use power to improve our lives? **They have more power than humans so they can accomplish more work in a given period of time.**

## Taking it further

- Why is a car more powerful than a bicycle? **Its engine is able to use fuel to perform more work in a given period of time than the muscles of your legs can; in this case that work is transporting a person a greater distance in a given period of time.**
- When a car is moving your body, the car is actually performing more work than when you walk the same distance. Why? **The car must move its own mass as well as yours.**

## Challenge: Calculating Power

- Which appliance will run the longest? **The one with the lowest power requirement. Probably your computer.**

- Which appliance will run the shortest period of time? **The one with the highest power requirement. Probably your car.**

<table>
<tr><td>QUIZ<br>**1**</td><td></td></tr>
</table>

# Mechanical Forces

### Lessons 1–8

**Match each term with its definition.**

1. _D_ The study of moving objects
2. _F_ Ability to perform work
3. _A_ Force times distance
4. _C_ Stored energy
5. _B_ Energy being used
6. _G_ Movement of mass in a certain direction
7. _I_ A push or pull
8. _J_ A continuous pull
9. _E_ Force that resists movement
10. _H_ Work done during a certain period of time

**Define the following terms.**

11. Law of conservation of energy: **Energy cannot be created or destroyed; it can only change form.**

12. Law of conservation of momentum: **Changes of momentum in an isolated system must be equal.**

## Challenge questions

13. A 70 kg skydiver is in an airplane at 1,500 meters above the earth. What is his potential energy? **PE =mgh = 70 kg x 9.8 m/s$^2$ x 1,500 m = 1,029,000 J.**

14. After jumping out of the plane, the skydiver is falling at 40 meters per second. What is his kinetic energy? **KE = ½ mv$^2$ = ½ x 70 kg x 40 m/s x 40 m/s = 56,000 J.**

15. Does he still have potential energy? **Yes. As long as he is above the ground he has potential energy. Some of the potential energy has been converted to kinetic energy, but not all.**

16. List two ways that physical laws are different from other laws. **Physical laws are designed by God not man, they cannot be broken or changed, they apply throughout the whole universe.**

17. If a car has a mass of 2,000 kg and is moving at 20 km/hr what is its momentum? **p = 2,000 kg x 20 km/hr = 40,000 kg-km/hr.**

18. If a plane is flying north at 400 miles per hour and there is a wind from the west at 20 miles per hour, describe the net forces acting on the plane. **The force of the engines is moving the plane north and the force of the wind is moving the plane east. The net force would be a movement to the northeast.**

19. Describe how friction can be reduced in a machine. **Adding lubricants such as oil, making the pieces very smooth, or using materials that easily slide against each other.**

20. How much work is done if a box weighing 100 newtons is lifted from the ground into the bed of a truck that is 2 meters off the ground? **W = F X D = 100 newtons X 2 meters = 200 newton-meters.**

# Unit 2
# Simple Machines

# 9 Simple Machines

Working for us

## Supply list

Machines and tools you have around your house

## Supplies for Challenge

Research materials for a machine of your choice

## Mechanical Advantage:

- Some possible simple machines you might have in your house include:

  Inclined planes: **Staircase, ramp, kitchen knives, pocket knife, scissors, axe.**

  Levers: **Anything with wheels and axle, garage door opener with pulleys, bicycle (wheels and gears), broom, nut cracker, scissors.**

## What did we learn?

- What are the two simple machines on which all machines are based? **The inclined plane and the lever.**

- Why are simple machines useful? **They allow us to move objects with less force.**

- What is mechanical advantage? **The reduction in force needed to move an object.**

- How do we "pay" for mechanical advantage? **The force must be applied over a longer distance.**

## Taking it further

- How does the work involved in moving a piano up a ramp compare with the work needed to lift it straight up the same distance? **The total work is the same, but the effort needed at any given moment is less using the ramp.**

- When might someone choose not to use a simple machine's mechanical advantage? **A very strong man might think it is not too much effort to lift a heavy box, whereas a child might need to use a ramp to move it. Another example might be if a hiker is in a hurry and would rather put forth the effort to climb straight up the hill, rather than take the longer route.**

# 10 Inclined Planes

Sliding it up

## Supply list

Piece of wood or cardboard at least 4 feet long

Block of wood with hook from lesson 6

Rubber band and ruler (or spring scale if available)

Copy of "Inclined Planes" worksheet

## Inclined Planes worksheet

- **Lifting the block straight up requires the most force. The longer ramp requires the least amount of force to move the block. M.A. of ramp 1: 3/2 = 1.5; M.A. of ramp 2: 4/2 = 2.**

## What did we learn?

- What is an inclined plane? **Essentially, it is a ramp.**
- Why do people use inclined planes? **It requires less force to move the same amount of mass up to a particular height, or you can move more mass with the same amount of force.**
- What is mechanical advantage? **It is the advantage you gain in reduced force required.**
- How do you "pay" for mechanical advantage? **You must move the object over a longer distance.**

## Taking it further

- What is the mechanical advantage of a ramp that is 50 meters long and has a height of 10 meters?
- **M.A. = Length/Height = 50/10 = 5. This means that it takes 5 times less force to move an object up the ramp than it does to lift it directly up 10 meters.**
- List several examples of where you see ramps or inclined planes at work. **Many buildings have ramps for handicapped people; manufacturing plants use ramps to move products; escalators and stairs are modified ramps, etc.**

# Wedges & Screws

## Divide and conquer

## Supply list

Paper

Cardboard

2 pencils

Tape

Optional—with adult supervision:

Knives

Scissors

Hatchet

## Supplies for Challenge

2 or more screws with different threads

Copy of "Comparing Screws" worksheet

Screwdriver      Ruler

Block of wood

## Understanding Screws

- Which pencil has closer stripes? Which ramp has the greater mechanical advantage? **The longer ramp has a greater mechanical advantage so its stripes will be closer together.**
- Which pencil did you have to turn the most times? **The one with the longer ramp.**
- If these were actual screws, which one would be hardest to drive into a piece of wood? **The one with the shortest ramp.**

## What did we learn?

- What is a wedge? **Two inclined planes placed bottom to bottom.**
- How are wedges used in tools? **Wedges are usually used as cutting edges. The inclined planes increase mechani-**

cal advantage, making it easier to cut or split different materials.

- What is a screw? **An inclined plane wrapped around a cylinder or cone.**
- How are screws used? **The inclined plane makes it easier to drive the screw into materials to hold them together.**
- What is the pitch of a screw? **The distance between the threads along the side of the screw.**

## Taking it further

- Which will be easier to drive into a piece of wood, a screw with 10 threads per inch or a screw with 15 threads per inch? **The one with 15 threads per inch.**
- Which of the above screws will go into the wood faster, assuming you have enough force to drive them both? **The one with 10 threads per inch.**
- Name at least two items with wedges that have not been mentioned in the lesson. **Drill bits, can opener, wood plane, metal or wire cutters, surgical instruments, sewing needles, etc.**

## Challenge: Comparing Screws worksheet

- **The screw with close threads should be easiest to drive. The screw that is harder to drive will go further into the wood. The distance between the threads is the pitch. The greater the pitch the greater the force needed to drive the screw, but also the greater the distance the screw will go with each turn.**

# 12 Levers

## Seesaw

## Supply list

Yardstick or meter stick      Block of wood

Small box      Ruler

## Supplies for Challenge

Copy of "Law of Moments" worksheet

## Experimenting with Levers

### Experiment 1:

- Move the fulcrum so that it is 12 inches (30 cm) from the box. Was it easier or harder to lift the box? **It will be easier.**

- Place the fulcrum 6 inches (15 cm) from the box and repeat. Was it easier or harder to lift the box this time? **Again, it is easier.**

- Try placing the fulcrum 24 inches (70 cm) from the box. Push down and lift the box. Was it harder this time? **Not only was it hard to lift the box, but you actually had to apply more force than if you just lifted the box without the lever. This may seem like a waste of effort; however, there are instances in which this type of lever system is useful.**

### Experiment 2:

- Which moved farther, your hand or the box? **Your hand moved much farther than the box did.**

- How does the distance your hand moved compare to the distance the box moved in each instance? **When the fulcrum is close to the box your hand moves more than the box does. When the fulcum is far away from the box, your hand moves less than the box does.**

- Can you think of a reason why you might want to have the fulcrum at 24 inches from the box now? **If moving the box a large distance is worth the extra effort, it might be worth using a lever where the fulcrum is closer to the effort than to the resistance.**

## What did we learn?

- What is a lever? **A stiff bar rotating about a fixed point.**

- How does a lever provide mechanical advantage? **It allows you to apply a smaller force over a greater distance.**

- Define each of the following terms: effort arm, resistance, effort, fulcrum. **The effort arm is the stiff bar; the resistance is the weight being moved; the effort is the force being applied to move the resistance; the fulcrum is the point about which the effort arm rotates.**

## Taking it further

- How does the distance principle apply to levers? **In order to reduce the force needed, the effort is applied over a greater distance than the distance the weight is moved.**

- Give an example where you might want to apply a large force over a short distance in order to move an object over a large distance. **One example is a catapult.**

- When using a lever, do you do less work than if you lifted the object without the lever? **You might think that because it is easier to lift the object with a lever, you are doing less work. However, if you recall from lesson 7, work is force applied over a distance. When you use a lever you apply less force, but you apply it over a greater distance so you are doing the same amount of work; it just feels easier.**

## Challenge: Law of Moments worksheet

1. $300N \times 3m = 450N \times D_2$ so $D_2 = 900/450 = 2$ m and the M.A. = 2/3 or 0.667.

2. M.A. must be 3 = 150/50 so $D_2/D_1 = 3$. With a 4-meter long lever, the fulcrum must be placed so that $D_2$ is 3 times longer than $D_1$. If $D_1 = 1$ m then $150N \times 1m = 50N \times D_2$ so $D_2 = 150/50 = 3$ m; so the fulcrum should be 1 m from the box and the force should be applied 3 m from the fulcrum.

3. $900N \times 2m = W_2 \times 3m$ so $W_2 = 1800/3 = 600$ N and the M.A. = 3/2 or 1.5.

# 13 First-, Second-, & Third-Class Levers

What class are you in?

## Supply list

Copy of "Lever Classification" worksheet

## Supplies for Challenge

Copy of "Third-class Levers" worksheet

## Lever Classification worksheet

Scissors: **1st**

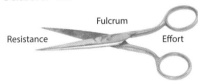

Tweezers: **3rd**

Nutcracker: **2nd**

Wheelbarrow: **2nd**

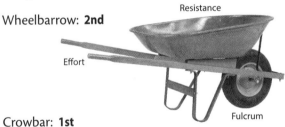

Crowbar: **1st**

Catapult: **3rd**

Chop saw: **2nd**

Shovel:

**(1st if you are pushing down with the back hand;**     **3rd if you are pulling up with the front hand.)**

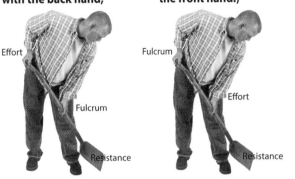

Door/hinge: **2nd**

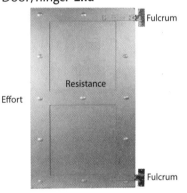

## What did we learn?

- Explain where the resistance, fulcrum, and effort are with respect to each other for each class of lever. **First-class: fulcrum between resistance and effort; second-class: resistance between fulcrum and effort; third-class: effort between fulcrum and resistance.**

- Which class(es) of levers allow you to apply less effort to move an object? **First- and second-class.**

- Which class(es) of levers allow you to move an object over a greater distance by applying more force? **Third-class.**

## Taking it further

- Which class(es) of levers will have a mechanical advantage less than 1? Which will be greater than 1? **Third-class will be less than 1; first- and second-class will be greater than 1.**
- What kind of lever might you use if you want to prune a tree? **Pruning shears are a first-class lever.**
- What class of lever is a pencil? **Third-class—The effort is applied below the fulcrum, which is where the pencil rests against your hand. The resistance is the friction between the pencil and the paper.**
- What advantage does a pencil give you? **Small movements of your finger result in greater movements of the end of the pencil so your hand doesn't get tried as easily and so you can write more quickly.**

## Challenge: Third-class Levers worksheet

- Lobster: **Small movements of the muscles allow the pinchers to move a larger amount. This allows the animal to quickly catch food or defend itself from predators. Resistance is whatever is caught in the pincers, fulcrum – is the joint where pincers are attached, effort is applied where the muscles are attached.**
- Chopsticks: **Small movements of your fingers cause the ends of the chopsticks to move a larger amount. This allows for great dexterity in eating without tiring your fingers. Resistance is the food being picked up between the ends of the chopsticks, fulcrum is where the chopsticks rest against your hand, effort is the pressure applied by your fingers.**
- Shears: **The blades move a much greater amount compared to the movement of your hand, allowing you to cut more wool in a shorter period of time than with traditional scissors. Keeps your hand from becoming tired as quickly because you are using smaller movements but requires stronger gripping muscles. Resistance is the wool being cut, fulcrum is the end of the shears, effort is the pressure applied in the center by your hand.**

# 14 Wheels & Axles

## Getting things moving

## Supply list

Bicycle (You can use the picture in the student manual if no bicycle is available, but it will be much easier with an actual bike.)

## Supplies for Challenge

Rubber band  Spring scale (optional)

Block of wood with hook from lesson 6

Several smooth, round pencils

Research materials on the development of the spoked wheel

## Examining Wheels

- What is the mechanical advantage of the pedals to the chain? **Divide the distance from the pedal by the distance from the chain.**
- Now examine the rear wheel of the bicycle. Measure the distance from the chain to the center of the rear axle. And measure the distance from the edge of the wheel to the center of the axle. What is the mechanical advantage at the rear wheel? **Remember, it will be less than 1. The large mechanical advantage of the pedals/gear system increases the effective force of your legs. The small mechanical advantage of the gear/rear wheel system uses that force and increases the distance the wheel moves so the bike moves a much longer distance than your legs move.**

## What did we learn?

- A wheel and axle is a more complex version of which simple machine? **The lever.**
- What are the main reasons for using a wheel and axle instead of a regular lever? **It allows the effort to be applied continuously so the resistance can continuously be moved. Also, a wheel reduces friction.**
- How does a wheel and axle increase mechanical advantage? **It allows you to apply the force at a greater distance than the resistance.**

## Taking it further

- How does a potter's wheel help the potter? **The wheel allows the potter to apply a force with his/her foot at** a greater distance from the center of the wheel than where the clay is. This causes the clay to spin and allows the potter to apply pressure on all sides of the clay.

# Gears

## Connecting wheels together

### Supply list

Copy of "Gear Patterns"        Straight pins
Cardboard

### Supplies for Challenge

Research materials on gears

### Playing With Gears

- Activity 1: **A is larger than B so it should make B move more quickly than it is moving. B should cause A to rotate more slowly than it is moving.**

- Activity 2: **Gear C should move in the same direction as gear A and the opposite direction as gear B.**

- Activity 3: **The rack moves right or left as the gear rotates. The rack should move a shorter distance with gear B than with gear A for the same amount of rotation.**

### What did we learn?

- What is a gear? **A toothed wheel and axle.**
- What are some functions that can be achieved with gear systems? **Change of speed, change of direction,** transfer of mechanical advantage, and changing straight motion into rotational or vise-versa.

- In a gear system, in general, which will have the greater speed, the larger or smaller gear? **The smaller gear.**
- Which will have the greater force, the larger or smaller gear? **The larger gear.**

### Taking it further

- Why do most bicycles have more than one gear? **To efficiently use mechanical advantage when riding over different terrain. Gears allow you to apply less force going up a hill and more force on a flat road.**

- How does putting a bicycle into a higher gear, one where the larger gear is driving the smaller gear, help a cyclist? **It uses the larger force of the larger gear to make the smaller gear move more quickly, increasing the speed of the bike.**

- How does putting a bicycle into a lower gear, one where the smaller gear is driving the larger gear, help a cyclist? **It makes it easier to pedal. Although the bike will move more slowly, the effort to keep the bike moving is less in a lower gear.**

# Pulleys

## Wheels with ropes

### Supply list

Broom        Rope
1-gallon jug filled with water

### Experimenting with Pulleys:

#### Activity 1: 1 fixed pulley

- How much effort is required to lift the jug with the rope by pulling down compared to lifting it vertically with the rope without using the broom? **It should feel about the same. It may actually feel slightly harder because of the friction between the rope and the broom.**

#### Activity 2: 2 pulleys

- How much effort is required to lift the jug compared to experiment 1? **It should be less.**
- How do you pay for this reduced effort? **By having to pull the rope down twice as far as the distance the jug moves up.**

**Activity 3: 4 pulleys**

- Does it feel easier than just lifting the jug alone? **It should feel a lot easier.**
- How far do you have to pull on the rope to lift the jug 1 foot off the ground? **You should have to pull the rope about 4 feet.**
- What is the mechanical advantage of this system? **Four.**

## What did we learn?

- What is a pulley? **A grooved wheel over which a rope can move.**
- What type of simple machine does a pulley represent? **A lever.**
- How does a pulley system provide a mechanical advantage? **It allows you to pull a rope through a longer distance so the effort required is less.**

## Taking it further

- If someone wants to lift an object that is five times heavier than the person, what is the minimum number of pulleys needed in order for the person to be able to lift the object? **Theoretically, the person would need five pulleys. However, in reality the loss of effort due to friction would require at least six pulleys.**
- How might a pulley system have been used in medieval warfare? **Pulleys were used to pull back catapult systems as well as crossbows and trebuchets.**

## Challenge: Mechanical Advantage

- For each set up, what is the mechanical advantage and with how much force would the person have to pull down on the rope in order to lift a 125 newton box?
  - A. M.A. = 1 so Force = 125 newtons.
  - B. M.A. = 3 so Force = 125/3 = 41.7 newtons
  - C. M.A. = 4 so Force = 125/4 = 31.3 newtons
  - D. M.A. = 5 so Force = 125/5 = 25 newtons
- How much rope would he have to pull though the system to lift the box 2 feet?
  - A. 2 feet
  - B. 6 feet
  - C. 8 feet
  - D. 10 feet
- What can be done to minimize this friction? **Make the pulleys out of smooth materials such as shiny metal or smooth plastic. Make the rope out of smooth material such as nylon. Put a lubricant (oil or grease) between the pulley and its axle.**
- What do you think is the purpose of the grooves in the pulleys? **To hold the rope in place so it does not slip off.**
- How do these grooves affect the amount of friction the pulley experiences? **The deeper the grooves the more contact the rope has with the pulley so the more friction is experiences.**
- What can be done to the grooves to minimize friction? **Make them shallow. However, there is a trade-off between increasing friction which requires more force and the stability that the deeper grooves provide.**

# QUIZ 2

# Simple Machines

## Lessons 9–16

**Short answer:**

1. What are the two simple machines that all other machines are based on? **Inclined plane, lever.**

2. For each class of lever, indicate where the resistance, effort, and fulcrum are found:
   a. First-class: The _**fulcrum**_ is between the _**effort**_ and the _**resistance**_.
   b. Second-class: The _**resistance**_ is between the _**fulcrum**_ and the _**effort**_.
   c. Third-class: The _**effort**_ is between the _**fulcrum**_ and the _**resistance**_.

3. List three ways that gears are used to change motion. **Direction, speed, linear to rotational.**

4. A pulley system with six pulleys has a mechanical advantage of _**six**_.

**Mark each statement as either True or False.**

5. _**T**_ Mechanical advantage is achieved by applying less force through a greater distance.

6. _**F**_ To make lifting an object easier, the fulcrum should be closer to the effort than the resistance.

7. _**F**_ A lever is a special inclined plane.

8. _**T**_ The distance between threads on a screw is called the pitch.

9. _**T**_ A screw is a special inclined plane.

10. _**T**_ A wedge increases your mechanical advantage.

11. _**F**_ All levers increase mechanical advantage.

12. _T_ Wheels decrease friction.

13. _F_ A pulley system allows you to pull the rope a shorter distance than you move the resistance.

14. _T_ A single fixed pulley has a mechanical advantage of 1.

15. _T_ Gears allow you to change the direction of a force.

## Challenge questions

**Short answer:**

16. Explain how friction affects the force needed to move an object up an inclined plane. **There is friction between the object being moved and the surface of the ramp, so the friction increases the force needed to move the object up the ramp.**

17. Explain how friction affects the force needed to lift an object with a rope and pulley. **There is friction between the rope and the pulley and between the axle and the pulley. This friction increases the force needed to lift the object.**

18. A box weighing 200 Newtons is placed on a first-class lever 3 meters from the fulcrum. How far from the fulcrum must you place a box weighing 400 Newtons in order to balance the lever? **$W_1D_1 = W_2D_2$ so $D_2 = W_1D_1/W_2$, $D_2 = 200 \times 3/400 = 1.5$ meters.**

19. Explain why rolling friction is less than sliding friction. **Rolling objects have only a small part in contact with the surface over which they are rolling for a short period of time.**

20. What is the mechanical advantage for a block and tackle systems with 3 pulleys? **Three.**

# Kinematics

## 17 Kinematics

### How do things move?

### Supply list

Wagon                                    Stuffed Animal

### Supplies for Challenge

Copy of "Frame of Reference" worksheet

### Frame of Reference

- How did the wagon appear to move? **Moving past you from left to right.**

- How did the stuffed animal appear to move? **Also, past you from left to right.**

- You sit in the wagon and have someone pull you over the same path. How does the wagon appear to move now? **Be sure to look only at the wagon. It should not appear to be moving because you are moving at the same speed and along the same path as the wagon.** How does the stuffed animal appear to move? **It should appear to move past you just as before.**

### What did we learn?

- What is kinematics? **The study of how things move.**

- What is frame of reference? **The point of view from which you are making your observations.**

- What is relative motion? **Motion must be described with respect to another object, generally compared to the observer.**

### Taking it further

- Why is it important to define your frame of reference when discussing motion? **Motion is different from different points of view, or different frames of reference.**

- If an observer were outside the Milky Way Galaxy and could observe the earth, what types of motion would the earth appear to be making? **The earth would be rotating on its axis and revolving around the sun. Also, the whole galaxy is spinning so the earth would be spinning with the galaxy as well as moving through the universe.**

- If a child on a moving train is tossing a ball and catching it, how does the ball appear to move from the child's point of view? **It moves up and down.**

- How does the ball appear to move to an observer standing on the ground outside the train? **The ball appears to move in arcs as it moves forward at the speed of the train as well as up and down.**

### Challenge: Frame of Reference worksheet

#### Example A:

1. From the boy's point of view, how fast is the airplane moving? **300 mph.**

2. From the boy's point of view, how fast is the bird moving? **10 mph.**

3. From the pilot's point of view, how fast is the boy moving? **300 mph.**

4. From the bird's point of view, how fast is the airplane moving? **290 mph.**

#### Example B:

1. How does the earth appear to move to the observer on the moon? **Rotates on its axis.**

2. How does the moon appear to move to the observer on the earth? **Revolves around the earth.**

3. How does the sun appear to move to the observer on the moon? **Revolves around the earth and moon together.**

4. How does the sun appear to move to the observer on the earth? **Revolves around the earth.**

5. How do the stars appear to move to the observer on the moon? **Revolve around the earth and moon together.**

6. How do the stars appear to move to the observer on the earth? **Revolve around the earth.**

# 18 Speed & Velocity

## How fast are you going?

## Supply list

Meter stick or tape measure

Stopwatch                   Tape or sidewalk chalk

Compass

## Supplies for Challenge

Copy of "Vectors" worksheet

## What did we learn?

- What is the definition of speed? **The rate at which something moves with respect to another object—or the distance covered in a given period of time.**
- What are the standard units for speed? **Meters per second.**
- How is velocity different from speed? **Velocity includes a direction as well as a rate.**

## Taking it further

- Why is it important to know an object's velocity instead of just its speed? **You don't know where an object ends up without knowing what direction it is moving.**
- What kind of instruments might be needed to measure speed and velocity? **To measure speed you need to be able to measure distance and time, so you might need a tape measure, ruler, or maybe even surveying equipment to measure distance. Then, to measure time, you need some type of stopwatch. To measure velocity, you also need to measure direction, so a compass or even a Global Positioning System might be useful. Other more sophisticated instruments are also available such as speedometers and air-speed gauges.**

## Challenge: Vectors worksheet

- Problem 1: At what speed and in which direction is the saucer moving? **14 mph heading east.**
- Problem 2: At what speed and in which direction does the ball actually move? **39 mph heading southwest. (This is an idealized calculation and doesn't take wind resistance into account.)**

# 19 Acceleration

## Speeding up

## Supply list

8-foot long 2x4 or other long piece of wood

Cardboard                   Stopwatch

Toy car                     Meter stick

Tape

## Supplies for Challenge

Copy of "Acceleration" worksheet

## What did we learn?

- What is acceleration? **The rate at which the velocity of an object changes.**
- What is the difference between acceleration and deceleration? **Acceleration is when the speed/velocity of an object is increasing. Deceleration is when the speed/velocity of an object is decreasing, also referred to as negative acceleration.**
- What causes an object to accelerate? **An additional force in the direction of the velocity.**
- What causes an object to decelerate? **A force opposing the motion of the object.**

## Taking it further

- When a runner is in a sprint race, is there a time when the runner is neither accelerating or decelerating? **When the runner has reached his maximum speed and has not yet begun to slow down, probably just before reaching the finish line.**

- What happens to the speed of an object that is accelerating? **Its speed is increasing.**

## Challenge: Acceleration worksheet
- **Gravity is a constant force, so you would expect the line to be straight unless some other force were introduced.**

# 20 Theory of Relativity

## Is everything relative?

## Supply list

Paper                    Markers

## What did we learn?

- Who developed the Special Theory of Relativity? **Albert Einstein.**
- What are some main ideas of the Special Theory of Relativity? $E = mc^2$; **time slows down as you approach the speed of light; mass increases as you approach the speed of light; nothing can go faster than the speed of light.**

## Taking it further
- Why is it difficult and likely impossible for an object to travel at the speed of light? **The mass of the object increases as it approaches the speed of light, so larger and larger forces are needed to accelerate the object to the speed of light.**
- If it were possible to travel at or near the speed of light, who would age faster, a person on earth or a person traveling in a rocket near the speed of light? **The person on earth would age faster because time slows down as you approach the speed of light.**

## QUIZ 3 Kinematics

### Lessons 17–20

**Choose the best answer.**

1. _A_ The study of how things move is called _____.
2. _B_ When observing motion, your point of view is determined by your _____.
3. _D_ Distance over time is called _____.
4. _B_ Velocity indicates speed as well as _____.
5. _B_ _____ describes how fast your speed is changing.
6. _A_ Changes in motion are caused by _____.
7. _C_ A force in the same direction as the object's motion will result in _____.
8. _D_ The Special Theory of Relativity was proposed by _____.
9. _B_ The Special Theory of Relativity shows that mass can be converted into _____.
10. _C_ The _____ does not depend on your frame of reference.

## Challenge questions

**Mark each statement as either True or False.**

11. _F_ The speed of a moving object is independent of the observer's frame of reference.
12. _F_ The stars would appear to move the same way to an observer on earth as they would to an observer on Uranus.
13. _T_ A vector can be used to represent the velocity of a moving object.
14. _F_ The length of a vector represents the direction an object is moving.
15. _T_ Experiments have been conducted that support the special theory of relativity.
16. _T_ $E = mc^2$ is part of the special theory of relativity.

# Unit 4
# Dynamics

## 21 First law of motion

Inertia

### Supply list

| | |
|---|---|
| Wagon or small cart | Playing card |
| Ball | Coin |
| Cup | |

### Supplies for Challenge

| | |
|---|---|
| Unshelled hard-boiled egg | Unshelled raw egg |

### What did we learn?

- What is inertia? **The tendency of an object to remain in its current state; either at rest or in motion.**
- What is Newton's first law of motion? **An object at rest tends to stay at rest and an object in motion tends to stay in motion until acted upon by an outside force.**

### Taking it further

- How will an object move if the forces acting on it are balanced—they are equal but in opposite directions? **It will not move.**
- When you jump you come down in about the same place on the floor. Since the earth is rotating on its axis, why don't you land in a different place as the earth moves under you? **You have inertia that keeps you moving at the same speed and in the same direction as the earth.**
- Since a stopped car wants to stay at rest, what force makes a car move? **The force created by the engine that turns the wheels.**
- Is more gasoline needed to get a car moving to begin with, or to keep the car moving at a constant speed? **More gas is needed to get the car moving because you must overcome the car's inertia. Once the car is moving, the gas is needed to overcome the forces of air resistance and friction, but the car itself tends to keep moving.**

### Challenge: Balanced Forces

- **There are many examples of balanced forces. With a hanging flower pot, the hook on the roof is pulling up with the same force that gravity is pulling down.**
- **To test the eggs you can spin each egg on a table then quickly stop the egg with your hand and release it. The hardboiled egg will stop spinning, but the raw egg will begin spinning again because of the inertia of the liquid inside the shell.**

## 22 Second Law of Motion

It's all about force

### Supply list

| | |
|---|---|
| Pair of rollerskates | Hammer |
| Can of food | Masking tape |

### Supplies for Challenge

Copy of "Applying the Second Law of Motion" worksheet

## What did we learn?

- What is the equation that expresses Newton's second law of motion? **F = m x a; force = mass x acceleratrion.**
- What is another name for the second law of motion? **The law of acceleration.**
- If the same force is applied to two objects with different masses, what will be the effect on their accelerations? **The object with the smaller mass will accelerate faster than the object with the greater mass.**
- If you wish to increase the acceleration of an object, how must the force change? **It must increase.**

## Taking it further

- How can you reduce the amount of force needed to accelerate an object? **You can only reduce the force if you are able to reduce the object's mass.**
- When might it be desirable to reduce mass to increase acceleration? **You might need to reduce mass on a rocket so it will be able to escape the earth's gravity using a certain sized engine. Pioneers had to reduce the mass in their wagons when their animals became weaker and could no longer pull with as much force.**

- How might a bicycle racer reduce the mass of her bicycle in order to increase acceleration? **Racing bikes are often made of very light materials. Also, some racing bikes have holes drilled into the frames to decrease their mass.**
- How does a bicycle racer increase the force he exerts on the pedals of the bike? **By training every day and increasing the size of his/her leg muscles or by standing on the pedals so his/her whole weight is pushing on them.**

## Challenge: Applying the Second Law of Motion worksheet

1. **F = 1,000 kg x 10 m/s² = 10,000 N**
2. **F = 2,000 kg x 10 m/s² = 20,000 N**
3. **Twice as much force is required since the mass is twice as large.**
4. **F = 2,000 kg x 5 m/s² = 10,000 N**
5. **The force is half as much since the acceleration is cut in half.**
6. **Other uses include jet engines and rocket engines, roller coasters, ballistics, etc.**

# 23 Third law of motion

## Equal and opposite

## Supply list

2 pairs of inline skates, rollerskates, or chairs with rollers

Balloon

## Supplies for Challenge

Research materials on helicopters and jet engines

## What did we learn?

- What is Newton's third law of motion? **For every action there is an equal and opposite reaction.**
- How can reactions be both equal and opposite? **The reaction is equal in force/strength and opposite in direction.**

## Taking it further

- How does a rifle demonstrate Newton's third law of motion? **When a bullet is fired out of the rifle there is an equal reaction in the opposite direction called the "kick" of the rifle, which is the rifle moving quickly backward.**

- How might you reduce the "kick" of a rifle? **Many rifles have a recoil reaction where the butt of the gun contains a spring or hydraulic cylinder that absorbs the energy of the kick and releases it more slowly, so you don't bruise your shoulder. Heavy barrels and the type of action also reduce the recoil.**

## Challenge: Aviation Research

- **Jet engines push air through them, causing the airplane to move forward. Helicopter blades push down on the air causing the air to push up on them, thus lifting the helicopter.**

# 24 Gravity

## It's pulling you down

## Supply list

Heavy book                    Piece of paper
Pen

## Supplies for Challenge

Scientific calculator
Copy of "Gravitational Force" worksheet

## What did we learn?

- What is gravity? **It is the force that all objects exert on each other.**
- What two factors affect the strength of gravitational pull? **The mass of the objects and the distance between them.**
- Who defined the laws of motion and the law of gravitation? **Sir Isaac Newton.**

## Taking it further

- Why can't you feel gravitational pull from other people? **Gravitational pull is a relatively weak force and people do not have enough mass to exert a large enough force to feel.**
- Since the earth is slightly flattened at the poles, do people at the North Pole experience more, less, or the same gravitational pull as people at the equator? **Since gravity is a function of distance from the center of the earth, and the earth is slightly flatter and therefore closer to the center of the earth at the poles, people at the poles experience slightly more gravity than people at the equator. Note however, that the difference is very small and not noticeable.**
- Do people in tall skyscrapers experience more or less gravity than people on the ground? **The people in tall building are slightly farther away from the center of the earth so they would experience slightly less gravitational pull. However, the difference is so tiny that you cannot tell there is a difference without extremely sensitive instruments.**
- What is the strength of the gravitational pull on your body? **It is equal to your weight.**
- Would the strength of the gravitational pull be more or less if you were on the moon? Why? **The moon is much smaller than the earth so its gravitational pull is less. The moon's gravity is about 1/6 that of the earth's.**

## Challenge: Gravitational Force worksheet

- Problem 1. $F = Gm_1m_2/d^2 = 6.6 \times 10^{-11} \times 80 \text{ kg} \times 1{,}000 \text{ kg} /100 \text{ m}^2 = 5.3 \times 10^{-8} \text{ N.}$
- Problem 2. $F = Gm_1m_2/d^2 = 6.6 \times 10^{-11} \times 80 \text{ kg} \times 2{,}000 \text{ kg} /100 \text{ m}^2 = 1.1 \times 10^{-7} \text{ N}$; the force is twice as strong since the mass has doubled.
- Problem 3. $F = Gm_1m_2/d^2 = 6.6 \times 10^{-11} \times 80 \text{ kg} \times 2{,}000 \text{ kg} /25 \text{ m}^2 = 4.2 \times 10^{-7} \text{ N}$; the force is four times larger since the distance has been halved, but is squared in the equation.

  Distance has a greater influence since it is a squared function in the equation.

  The earth has more influence, even though it has a much smaller mass than the sun, because it is so much closer than the sun.

# 25 Falling Bodies

## Are you falling?

## Supply list

Egg
Craft supplies

## Supplies for Challenge

Several different balls          Tape
Shoe box lid                    Bucket
Thin cardboard

### The Great Egg Drop

- If you are successful, try dropping it from a greater height. Does the height make a difference? Why/why not? **The longer an object falls the faster is moves, thus giving it more momentum. So your egg will need more protection the greater the height from which is it dropped.**

### What did we learn?

- What did Galileo discover about the speed and acceleration of falling bodies? **He discovered that all falling bodies accelerate at the same rate so their speeds will be the same when dropped from the same height.**
- What is terminal velocity? **The maximum speed that a falling body can reach—about 177 feet/second on earth.**
- Why do falling objects have a terminal velocity? **Air resistance keeps them from accelerating indefinitely.**

### Taking it further

- How was Galileo's approach to science different from other scientists? **He believed in experimenting to test his theories.**
- Why is it important to test your scientific theories? **Sometimes what seems obvious at first is not correct** when tested. Experimentation can show that something is lacking in your understanding of the situation.
- Can all theories be tested? **No, theories about how the earth was formed, how life began, or spiritual ideas are some theories that cannot be recreated or tested so they are not in the realm of science. Many other theories are outside the realm of science as well.**
- Which will hit the ground first, a bullet fired horizontally from a gun or a bullet dropped from the height of the gun? **They will hit the ground at the same time. Although the bullet fired from the gun will travel horizontally a great distance, the vertical distance is the same and the gravitational pull on the bullets is the same so the bullets will fall at the same rate. Try this experiment with two identical balls. Roll one ball quickly across a table. At the same instant the ball leaves the table, drop the second ball from the same height as the table. The balls will hit the ground at about the same time. There may be slight differences between when one ball is released versus the other ball, and the height, so there may be a slight difference in when they hit.**

### Challenge: Falling Balls

- **The balls should all land in the same spot because they are falling at the same rate.**

# 26 Center of Mass

## What is in the middle?

### Supply list

| | |
|---|---|
| Marble | Ruler |
| 2 canning jar rings | Cardboard or wood |
| Roll of masking tape | Stack of books |

### Supplies for Challenge

| | |
|---|---|
| Tagboard or thin cardboard | Ruler |
| Hole punch | Tack or push pin |
| String | |

### Understanding Center of Mass

- Which object has the mass closest to the center? **The marble.**
- Which object has the mass farthest from the center? **The rings or the tape, depending on their size.**

### What did we learn?

- What is the center of mass of an object? **The point at which the mass seems to be concentrated—the point at which gravity is pulling down.**
- What is another name for center of mass? **Center of gravity.**

### Taking it further

- Is the center of gravity always in the center of an object? **Not necessarily; it depends how the mass is arranged in the object.**
- What will the effect be of placing a piece of clay inside a ball against one side? **This will cause the center of mass to shift from the center toward that side of the ball, so when the ball is rolled it will stop with the weighted side down. Many children's toys use this concept to make objects that tip but do not fall over.**

# Dynamics

### Lessons 21–26

**Write out each of the following laws.**

1. Newton's first law of motion: **An object at rest will remain at rest and an object in motion will remain in motion unless acted upon by an outside force.**

2. Newton's second law of motion: **The force required to move an object is equal to the object's mass multiplied by its acceleration, or F = m x a.**

3. Newton's third law of motion: **For every action there is an equal and opposite reaction.**

4. Law of universal gravitation: **Any two bodies attract each other with a force proportional to the product of their masses and inversely proportional to the square of the distance between them.**

5. Number the steps of the scientific method in the order that Galileo did them to prove that falling bodies all fall at the same rate.

   _1_ Thought about the problem

   _6_ Drew conclusions

   _3_ Devised a test/experiment

   _2_ Proposed a hypothesis/ possible solution

   _4_ Performed an experiment

   _5_ Compared results to hypothesis

6. How was Galileo's method different from Aristotle's method? **Galileo performed experiments; Aristotle did not.**

**Fill in the blank with the correct term.**

7. _**Inertia**_ is the tendency for an object to resist change.

8. Another name for the second law of motion is _**the law of acceleration**_.

9. _**Galileo**_ is considered the first modern scientist to perform experiments.

10. The two characteristics that affect the strength of gravitational pull are _**mass**_ and _**distance**_.

11. Center of mass is sometimes referred to as _**center of gravity**_.

## Challenge questions

**Mark each statement as either True or False.**

12. _**T**_ If forces are balanced an object will not move.

13. _**T**_ Newton's second law of motion is important in car design.

14. _**F**_ Force equals mass times velocity.

15. _**F**_ Helicopters do not use the action/reaction principle.

16. _**T**_ Jet engines push air out the back to move the airplane forward.

17. _**F**_ In the gravitational equation, replacing an object with one that is twice as massive results in a gravitational force that is half as strong.

18. _**T**_ In the gravitational equation, moving an object twice as far away results in a gravitational force that is four times weaker.

19. _**F**_ Heavier objects fall faster than lighter objects.

20. _**T**_ If a light ball and a heavy ball are rolled down the same ramp, they will land in the same location.

21. _**F**_ The center of mass is always in the center of an object.

# Unit 5
# Circular & Periodic Motion

## 27 Circular Motion
### Spinning around

### Supply list

Paper or Styrofoam cup    Scissors

String    Optional: gyroscope

Hole punch

### What did we learn?

- What causes an object flying through the air to move in an arc? **The force of gravity continuously pulling down causes it to change direction while the force propelling it causes it to travel in a straight line. These two forces combined cause the object to travel in an arc.**

- What causes an object to move in a circular path? **A force that continually changes the direction of the object by pulling or pushing it toward the center.**

- What is the name of the force that causes an object to move in a circle? **Centripetal force.**

### Taking it further

- What groups of people might need to understand ballistics? **Rocket designers and military strategists working with artillery, missiles, and guns are a few.**

- If you shoot a jet of water into the air, what shape would you expect the water to make and why? **If it is shot at an angle, it will make an arc. The force of the pump will make the water go in a straight line, but gravity will pull down on it as it moves, so it will form an arc.**

## 28 Motion of the Planets
### Our solar system

### Supply list

Tennis ball    String

### What did we learn?

- Why is Newton's law called the universal law of gravitation? **Because gravity applies to everything in the universe.**

- How does gravity affect the motion of the planets in our solar system? **Gravity pulls all of the planets toward the sun, thus changing their forward motion into circular motion.**

- What is the shape of a planet's orbit? **It is an ellipse, which is a stretched-out circle.**

### Taking it further

- Which objects in space are affected by the sun's gravity? **All objects in our solar system. Objects outside our solar system are too far away to be significantly affected by the sun's gravity, but may be affected by gravity from other stars or planets.**

- Do planets revolve around the sun at a constant speed? **No, because a planet moves in an ellipse, it is not a constant distance from the sun so the sun's gravitational pull is not constant. Therefore, the planet moves faster when it is closer to the sun and slower when it is farther away.**

# 29 Periodic Motion

## Can you keep time?

### Supply list

Metal Slinky®

### What did we learn?

- What is periodic motion? **Motion that happens over and over at a set rate.**
- Give three examples of periodic motion. **Circular motion, springs, and pendulums.**

- What is one invention that uses the periodic motion of springs and pendulums? **Clock.**

### Taking it further

- Why do the oscillations of a spring or pendulum eventually stop? **Friction resists the movement and forces some of the energy to be turned into heat.**

# 30 Pendulums

## Back and Forth

### Supply list

String                                  Tape

4 metal washers or nuts        Stopwatch

Copy of "Pendulum Data Sheet"

### Pendulum Data Sheet

- **The only change that should affect the period of the pendulum is its length. The longer the pendulum, the slower it swings and the longer the period will be. Varying the arc or the mass should not significantly affect the period.**

### What did we learn?

- What is a pendulum? **A mass on the end of a string or bar that swings back and forth.**
- Describe how the height from which the mass is dropped affects the period of the pendulum. **It does not affect it.**
- Describe how the mass of the pendulum affects the period of the pendulum. **It does not affect it.**

- Describe how the length of the pendulum affects the period of the pendulum. **The longer the pendulum the longer the period; the shorter the pendulum the shorter the period.**

### Taking it further

- How does what we learned about falling bodies relate to the period of pendulums? **Recall that heavy and light falling bodies fall at the same rate, so it makes sense that different weights of pendulums should fall at the same rate. You would expect that the weight would not affect the period of a pendulum based on these observations.**

### Challenge: Mapping the Earth

- **In areas that are closer to the center of the earth, the gravitational pull will be slightly stronger. So, the period of the pendulum will be slightly less than in areas that are farther away from the center of the earth. This difference can be used to map the surface of the earth. Equipment must be very sensitive, however.**

# Circular & Periodic Motion

Lessons 27–30

**Using the terms below, label the forces acting on each sphere.**

A: Force 1 —**Centripetal**    Force 2—**Forward momentum**

B: Force 1—**Forward momentum**    Force 2—**Gravity**

C: Force 1—**Forward momentum**    Force 2—**Gravity and centripetal (Gravity is the centripetal force.)**

**Short answer:**

1.  Which planet has the fastest orbit? **Mercury.**

2.  Which planet has the slowest orbit? **Neptune (Pluto is no longer considered a planet).**

3.  What kinds of heavenly bodies are affected by gravity? List at least three. **Planets, moons, comets, asteroids, stars, meteors.**

4.  Name two devices that have oscillations. **Springs, pendulums.**

5.  What characteristic of a pendulum affects its period? **Length.**

## Challenge questions

**Match each term with its definition.**

6.  _**A**_ One complete movement

7.  _**D**_ Changing between potential and kinetic energy

8.  _**G**_ The time for one complete cycle

9.  _**E**_ The number of cycles in 1 second

10.  _**F**_ The position about which the oscillation occurs

11.  _**B**_ The amount an object moves in each direction

12.  _**C**_ The process causing the oscillations to die down

# Use of Machines

## 31 Machines in History

### The early examples

### Supply list

Wooden blocks          Toothpicks

### Supplies for Challenge

Research materials for your chosen topic

### What did we learn?

- Which machines are believed to have been used by the Ancient Egyptians to build the pyramids? **Rollers—logs, which are similar to wheels; inclined planes—ramps.**
- Which machines are believed to have been used by the builders of Stonehenge? **Rollers and levers, and perhaps planks and ramps.**

### Taking it further

- What are some advantages of using modern machines to build structures? **Less time and fewer people are needed compared to using only simple machines.**
- Do modern machines make it possible to build stronger, more durable, or more beautiful buildings? **Not necessarily; some buildings built throughout history have been very strong and durable. Also, artists have made very beautiful buildings without modern machines.**
- If the Egyptians had the wheel, why didn't they use wheeled carts to move the large stones? **The stones were extremely heavy. The wheels may not have been strong enough to support the weight or they may have sunk into the sand and not been as efficient as logs.**

## 32 Machines in Nature

### How God designed it

### Supply list

Copy of "Machines in My Body" worksheet
Your body          Bubble gum
Book          Rolling chair

### Supplies for Challenge

Copy of "Animal Wedges" worksheet

### Machines in My Body

Activity 1: What class of lever is your finger in this situation? **3rd class.**

- Where is the effort, fulcrum, and resistance? **Effort – muscles in your hand attached in the middle of your finger; fulcrum – where your finger meets the table; resistance – book.**

Activity 2: What type of machine is your tongue during this activity? **A wedge – inclined plane.**

Activity 3: What class of lever is your body in this situation? **1st class.**

- Where is the effort, fulcrum, and resistance? **Effort – table pushing against your hands; fulcrum – your shoulders; resistance – your weight in the chair .**

Activity 4: What type or types of machines are your fingernails in this situation? **Lever and wedge – the shape of your fingernails allows the splinter to easily move up as the fingernails move down.**

- If you think they are a lever what class lever would they be? **3rd class – they are acting like tweezers.**

- If you think they are a lever where is the effort, fulcrum, and resistance? **Effort is in the middle of where your fingers meet; fulcrum it the top of where your fingers meet; resistance is the splinter.**

## What did we learn?

- What types of simple machines do the muscles and bones in animals represent? **Levers.**
- What common simple machine is found in the shape of many animal bodies? **Wedge.**

## Taking it further

- What is one reason why red blood cells are disc-shaped and smooth? **The round design of the cells works like a wheel to reduce friction and allows the cells to move freely through the blood vessels.**
- Explain why the shapes of teeth are helpful for biting into food. **The incisors and canine teeth are** wedge shaped, making it easier for them to cut into food.
- What shape does an eagle make with its body when it is diving? Why? **A wedge; the wedge shape allows the eagle to more easily overcome air resistance so it can dive faster.**

## Challenge: Animal Wedges worksheet

- Fish: **Body helps it move through the water.**
- Earthworm: **Head, tail help it move through dirt.**
- Mosquito: **Proboscis helps it penetrate skin.**
- Rat: **Nose/face helps it wriggle into tight spots.**
- Badger: **Nose/face helps it wriggle into the ground; nails help it dig tunnels.**
- Lion: **Claws for grasping and teeth for tearing and eating.**

# 33 Modern Machines
## How they work today

## Supply list

Copy of "Machine Identification" worksheet

## Machine Identification worksheet

Engine

levers

levers

gears

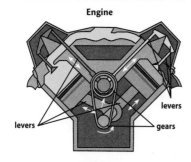

Clock

screws

levers

gears

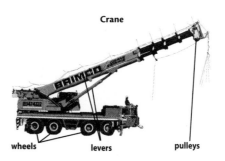

Crane

wheels

levers

pulleys

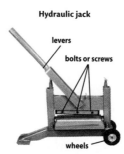

Hydraulic jack

levers

bolts or screws

wheels

## What did we learn?

- What are all modern machines comprised of? **A combination of simple machines.**
- Name several machines in your home. **Answers will vary.**

## Taking it further

- How would your life be different if you had no modern machines? **Answers will vary.**

## Challenge: Internal Combustion Engine

- **The automobile will not move until a force is applied by the engine. The pistons provide this force. This is the** first law of motion. The force produced by the moving pistons moves the mass of the car and causes it to accelerate. This is the second law of motion. The piston pushes down on the gas in the cylinder and the gas pushes back causing pressure inside the cylinder. This is the third law of motion.

- Gears and levers are used to move the pistons—turning a relatively small force into a greater force to compress the gas in the cylinder. This is mechanical advantage. Also the pistons move a relatively small amount but the gears and drive shaft move the wheels a greater amount, this is another example of mechanical advantage.

# 34 Using Simple Machines

## Putting it all together

## Final Project supply list

Depends on the design of your machine. Possible supplies include levers, gears, and pulleys.

## Supplies for Challenge

Research materials on famous physicists

## What did we learn?

- What are Newton's three laws of motion? **Fist law—An object at rest will remain at rest and an object in motion will remain in motion unless acted upon by an outside force. Second law—The force required to move an object is equal to the object's mass times its accelera-** tion. Third law—For every action there is an equal and opposite reaction.

- What is the difference between speed and velocity? **Velocity includes a direction.**
- What is the first law of thermodynamics? **Mass and energy cannot be created or destroyed; they can only change forms.**
- What is the law of conservation of momentum? **Changes of momentum in a closed system must be equal.**

## Taking it further

- What is your favorite machine? How does it demonstrate the laws listed here? **Answers will vary.**

# QUIZ 6 Use of Machines

## Lessons 31–34

**Short answer:**

1. Describe how ancient structures were built using simple machines. **They used logs as rollers, and used ramps and levers to move heavy objects.**
2. Describe how God designed plant structures to work like simple machines. **Roots are wedges, leaves have levers.**
3. Describe how God designed animal structures to work like simple machines. **Many animals have claws, beaks,** or other body parts shaped like wedges. Also, muscles and bones are levers.

4. Describe how God designed human body structures to work like simple machines. **There are many levers in the human body, especially with bones and muscles including the neck, ankle, and elbow.**

5. Explain how a blender uses simple machines to make chopping and blending easier. **A blender has gears that**

turn the blades, and the blades are wedge-shaped for cutting.

## Challenge questions

**Match each scientist with his major contribution to physics.**

6. _E_ Logical method for thinking about problems

7. _C_ Experimental testing of a hypothesis
8. _G_ War machines
9. _B_ Laws of motion
10. _F_ Planetary laws of motion
11. _D_ First accurate pendulum clock
12. _A_ Theory of relativity

FINAL EXAM

# Machines & Motion

### Lessons 1–34

**Match each term with its definition.**

1. _D_ Stored energy
2. _C_ Energy being used
3. _B_ A push or a pull
4. _A_ Tendency for an object to remain in its current state
5. _K_ Force toward the center of a circle
6. _E_ Force resisting movement
7. _F_ Force over a distance
8. _J_ Work done in a period of time
9. _G_ Speed in a particular direction
10. _L_ How much of something there is
11. _H_ The rate at which speed is increasing
12. _I_ The maximum velocity a falling object can achieve

**Identify the physical law described below.**

13. An object at rest tends to stay at rest, and an object in motion tends to stay in motion until acted upon by an outside force. **First law of motion.**

14. The momentum of a system after a collision must be the same as the momentum before the collision. **Law of conservation of momentum.**

15. Force is equal to mass times acceleration. **Second law of motion.**

16. Matter and energy cannot be created or destroyed; they can only change forms. **First law of thermodynamics, or laws of conservation of mass and conservation of energy.**

17. For every action, there is an equal and opposite reaction. **Third law of motion.**

18. The force of gravity is proportional to the masses of the objects and inversely proportional to the square of the distance between them. **Law of universal gravitation.**

19. Label each picture below with the type of simple machine shown.

1. **Lever**
2. **Gear/lever**
3. **Screw/inclined plane**
4. **Wheel/lever**

20. Identify each of the following as an example of either an inclined plane (IP) or a lever (L).

A. _IP_ Stairs
B. _L_ Shovel
C. _L_ Elevator
D. _IP_ Mountain road
E. _L_ Transmission
F. _L_ Clock gear

**Mark each statement as either True or False.**

21. _F_ It is possible to build a machine that never runs down.

22. _T_ The upward force of water on a ship is equal to the weight of the water displaced by the ship.

23. _F_ Friction is always destructive.

24. _F_ Holding a book above your head is more work than picking it up.

25. _T_ A car is more powerful than a bike if it helps you accomplish more work in less time.

26. _T_ Mechanical advantage is gained at the cost of distance.

27. _F_ Motion is independent of your frame of reference.

28. _T_ It is easier to change the direction of a light object than of a heavy object.

29. _F_ Heavier objects fall faster than lighter objects.

30. _T_ Longer pendulums swing more slowly than shorter pendulums.

31. _F_ For every action there is an equal in direction and opposite in strength reaction.

32. _T_ Galileo is considered to be the first modern scientist to experiment with and test his ideas.

33. _T_ The earth's center of mass is in the very core of the earth.

34. _F_ Newton invented gravity.

35. _T_ The movement of the planets obey Newton's laws of motion.

## Challenge questions

**Use the formulas below to help you in answering the following questions.**

36. How are physical laws different from legal laws? **Physical laws were made by God. They cannot be broken; they apply everywhere in the universe; this is not necessarily true of legal laws.**

37. Calculate the potential energy of a 50 kg boy sitting on the top of a 5 meter rock. **P.E. = 50 kg x 9.8 m/s² x 5 m = 2,450 J.**

38. Calculate the kinetic energy of a 1 kg ball traveling at 10 meters/second. **K.E. = 0.5 x 1 kg x 100 m²/s² = 50 J.**

39. Calculate the mechanical advantage of a first-class lever with the fulcrum 0.5 meter from the mass to be lifted and 2 meters from the end that you can push on. **M.A.=$D_1/D_2$=2m/0.5m=4.**

40. Give one reason why it might be important to know the center of mass of an object. **It may be necessary to know where an object's center of mass is so you know how it will react and move. For example, a car's center of mass must be low enough that it will not tip when rounding a corner.**

41. What is centripetal force? **Centripetal force is the force applied to an object to cause it to move in a circle.**

42. Explain why a pendulum would move differently on the moon than it does on earth. **It would not slow down like it does on earth because there is no air. It would move slower because the force of gravity is much less on the moon.**

# 35 Conclusion

God set everything in motion

## Supply list

Bible

# Resource Guide

Many of the following titles are available from Answers in Genesis (www.AnswersBookstore.com).

## Suggested Books

*Objects in Motion: Principles of Classical Mechanics* by Paul Fleisher—good explanation of many important physical principles

*Usborne Science Encyclopedia* by Kirsteen Rogers and others—great reference book for all ages

*Science and the Bible* Volumes 1–3 by Donald B. DeYoung—scientific demonstrations with Biblical truths

*Exploring the World of Physics* by John Hudson Tiner—Historical and biblical view of physics concepts

*Exploring the World of Mathematics* by John Hudson Tiner—Historical and biblical view of mathematics

*Invention Mysteries* and *More Invention Mysteries* by Paul Niemann—Fun "rest of the story" articles about many inventions

## Suggested Videos

*Newton's Workshop* by Moody Institute—Excellent Christian science series; several titles to choose from

## Field Trip Ideas

- Visit the Creation Museum in Petersburg, Kentucky.
- Hike up a hill or mountain and experiment with climbing straight up versus taking a zig zag path (an inclined plane).
- Visit a planetarium and learn more about the motion of the planets.
- Tour a local factory to see all of the simple and complex machines that are being used and built.

## Creation Science Resources

*Answers Book for Kids* Six volumes by Ken Ham with Cindy Malott and others—Answers children's frequently asked questions

*The New Answers Books 1–4* by Ken Ham and others—Answers frequently asked questions

*The Amazing Story of Creation* by Duane T. Gish—Gives scientific evidence for the creation story

*Creation Science* by Felice Gerwitz and Jill Whitlock—Unit study focusing on creation

*Creation: Facts of Life* by Gary Parker—Comparison of the evidence for creation and evolution

*The Young Earth* by John D. Morris—Lots of facts disproving old-earth ideas

# Master Supply List

The following table lists all the supplies used for *God's Design for the Physical World: Machines & Motion* activities. You will need to look up the individual lessons in the student book to obtain the specific details for the individual activities (such as quantity, color, etc.). The letter *c* denotes that the lesson number refers to the challenge activity. Common supplies such as colored pencils, construction paper, markers, scissors, tape, etc., are not listed.

| Supplies needed (see lessons for details) | Lesson |
|---|---|
| Balloons | 23 |
| Beads (large and small glass or plastic) | 4c |
| Bible | 35 |
| Bicycle | 14 |
| Box (small) | 7, 12 |
| Broom | 16 |
| Bubble gum | 32 |
| Bucket | 25c |
| Calculator | 4c, 24c |
| Canning jar rings | 26 |
| Cans | 4c |
| Coins (pennies, nickels) | 21 |
| Compass (illustration) | 2 |
| Compass (navigational) | 18 |
| Cup hook | 6 |
| Cups (paper or foam) | 27 |
| Dominoes | 4 |
| Eggs (hard-boiled and raw) | 21c, 25 |
| Gallon jug | 16 |
| Golf ball | 4, 25 |
| Gyroscope (optional) | 27 |
| Hammer | 22 |
| Marbles | 4, 25c, 26 |
| Masking tape | 18, 19, 22, 26, 30 |
| Modeling clay | 5 |

| Supplies needed (see lessons for details) | Lesson |
|---|---|
| Nuts or washers | 30 |
| Ping pong ball | 4, 25 |
| Playing card | 21 |
| Poster board/cardboard/tagboard | 11, 15, 19, 25c, 26c |
| Pulleys (optional) | 16, 34 |
| Rollerskates or inline skates | 22, 23 |
| Rolling chair | 32 |
| Rope | 5, 16 |
| Rubber bands | 2, 6, 10, 14c |
| Sandpaper | 6 |
| Scale (bathroom) | 5c, 7c |
| Screwdriver | 11c |
| Screws (with various threads) | 11c |
| Shoebox lid | 25c |
| Sidewalk chalk | 18 |
| Slinky® (metal) | 29 |
| Spring scale (optional) | 6, 10, 14c |
| Stopwatch | 18, 19, 30 |
| Straight pins | 15 |
| String | 1, 5, 26, 27, 28, 30 |
| Stuffed animal | 17 |
| Tack or push pin | 26c |
| Tennis ball | 1, 21, 25, 28 |
| Tennis racquet or baseball bat | 1 |
| Thread (spools) | 4c, 5 |
| Toothpicks | 31 |
| Wagon or cart | 17, 21 |
| Wood (for making a ramp) | 3, 10, 19, 26 |
| Wood (block) | 6, 11c, 12, 14, 31 |
| Yard stick/meter stick and ruler | 2, 4c, 6, 7c, 11, 12, 18, 19, 26 |

# Works Cited

"A. Einstein." http://www.aip.org/history/einstein/.

"Albert Einstein: Biography." http://nobelprize.org/physics/laureates/1921/einstein-bio.html.

"Albert Einstein." http://www-gap.dcs.st-and.ac.uk/~history/Mathematicians/Einstein.html.

"Angular Momentum." http://astrosun2.astro.cornell.edu/academics/courses/astro201/galaxies/angmo.htm.

"Archimedes." http://www.crystalinks.com/archimedes.html.

"Archimedes." http://www.shu.edu/projects/reals/history/archimed.html.

"Archimedes." https://www.cs.drexel.edu/~crorres/Archimedes/contents.html.

"Archimedes of Syracuse." http://scienceworld.wolfram.com/biography/Archimedes.html.

Ardley, Neil. *The Science book of Gravity.* San Diego: Gulliver Books, 1992.

Ardley, Neil. *The Science Book of Motion.* San Diego: Gulliver Books, 1992.

"Christiaan Huygens." http://www-groups.dcs.st-and.ac.uk/~history/Mathematicians/Huygens.html.

"Christian Huygens." http://inventors.about.com/library/inventors/bl_huygens.htm.

Clark, John O. *Physics Matters! Volume 2 Mechanics.* Danbury: Grolier Educational, 2001.

"Einstein's Wife: The Life of Mileva Meric Einstein." http://www.pbs.org/opb/einsteinswife/milevastory/index.htm.

Fleisher, Paul. *Objects in Motion: Principles of Classical Mechanics.* Minneapolis: Lerner Publications Company, 2002.

"Great Pyramid of Khufu." http://www.greatbuildings.com/buildings/Great_Pyramid.html.

Jenkins, John E., and George Mulfinger, Jr. *Basic Science for Christian Schools.* Greenville: Bob Jones University Press, 1983.

"Johannes Kepler." http://www.phy.hr/~dpaar/fizicari/xkepler.html.

"Johannes Kepler." www-groups.dcs.st-and.ac.uk/~history/Mathematicians/Kepler.html.

"Johannes Kepler: His Life, His Laws and Times." http://kepler.nasa.gov/johannes/#anchor779268.

Juettner, Bonnie. *Motion.* Detroit: Kid Haven Press, 2005.

Kerrod, Robin. *Force and Motion.* New York: Marshall Cavendish, 1994.

Lafferty, Peter. *Force & Motion.* New York: Dorling Kindersley Publishing, 1992.

Parker, Barry. *The Mystery of Gravity.* New York: Benchmark Books, 2003.

Parker, Steve. *Science Project Book of Mechanics.* New York: Marshall Cavendish Corporation, 1993.

"Perpetual Futility." http://www.lhup.edu/~dsimanek/museum/people/people.htm.

"Perpetual Motion?" http://www.besslerwheel.com/pm.html.

"Picking on Einstein." http://science.nasa.gov/headlines/y2005/28mar_gamma.xml.

"Stonehenge." http://www.britannia.com/history/h7.html.

VanCleave, Janice. *Physics for Every Kid.* New York: John Wiley & Sons, Inc., 1991.

Watson, Philip. *Super Motion.* New York: Lothrop, Lee & Shepard Books, 1982.

"What's the Story Behind Stonehenge?" http://ask.yahoo.com/ask/20010726.html.

"The Wheel Keeps Rotating." http://english.pravda.ru/science/19/94/379/12618_.html.

Wile, Jay L., and Marilyn M. Shannon. *The Human Body.* Cincinnati: Apologia Educational Ministries, Inc., 2001.